How Hard Can It Be?

Opportunities, Luck, Mistakes and Lessons:

The Story of Marcia's Den

Dedication

This book is dedicated first of all to my wife Marcia, who has always, unconditionally supported me through everything in our lives together. She has been the quiet guide and the glue for our family, which made all things possible.

How Hard Can It Be?

Opportunities, Luck, Mistakes and Lessons:

The Story of Marcia's Den

Contents

Table of Contents

Part One *8*
   In the Beginning: 8
   Saved by the Army: 17
   Target Shooting 24
   Karma, sort of: 26
   Transportation Troubles 30
   Victoria 33
   Chinese Takedown 38
   Our First Digs 40
   Motorcycles 46
   Surfing 49
   Stealing From the Police 53
   Taking On Water 60
   When To Run? 62

Part Two *68*

   A Tropical Island? 68

   Outdoor Activities 71

   The Cabin 79

   Our New Arrival 86

   Our Second New Arrival: 90

Part Three *94*

   Entrepreneurial Training 94

   Our First House 99

   The Hole 101

   The Trouble With Fire 104

   Finally Doing Well in School 105

   Marching 108

   Arm Wrestling 109

   The Worthless Chair 112

   Rocking Rocks 113

   The Pig 114

Part Four *116*

   Ending a Career 116

   Partnership 119

   The Landlord Business 128

   Welding 130

   Go Sell It on the Mountain 133

   The First Marcia's Den 139

   Tick Removal 141

   New Ups and Downs 143

The "Flip" 148
Dad 150

Part Five *155*
A New Door Opens 155
From Hobie to "Homie" 158
O'Boys 166
Sight Unseen 169
Knowledge is Power 171
The Trades 172
The Bad Feeling 176
Not Just the Water is Cold 179
The Seabird 181

Part Six *190*
Ending the Parties: 190
Graduation: 191
Power Union 192
Stepping Up Before Stepping Away 197
If You Can, You Can't 201
More Opportunities 203
Cameo 213
Marcia Gives Even More 215

Part Seven *217*
The Dreaded Restaurant 217
Dreary Winters 221
From Sail to Boathouse 224
Making Good on a Leaky Problem 227

Call of the U.S. 229

Drifting Apart 230

Part Eight *236*

A New Construction Project 236

The New Big Rig 238

The Start and End of Touring 240

Timing Is Everything 243

12-12-12 246

Changing Cars Midstream 249

From Water to Green 253

The Mobile Tombstone 261

In Closing 269

Part One

In the Beginning:

It seems I've always been in a hurry, always in a rush to get things done, and according to my mother, it started with me beginning the birth process before everyone was quite ready. I announced my entrance a bit early, and just got on with it.

I didn't know what to expect; after all, I was new in the world, but how hard could it be! Apparently some people take a lifetime to learn how to manage their situation, but I was sure I could take shortcuts that no one else had found and get there sooner!

From the beginning of my childhood I wanted results, but did everything I could to avoid the work required to get those results. When I heard what someone had toiled to achieve, I would immediately envision how I would magically arrive at the same place only without doing the work. My "work" would be finding the shortcut!

Dennis 1 year just July 1951

I was never prepared to just accept someone's advise; I had to challenge everything. I was going to do it my way, and if that didn't turn out right, then I'd make it right. As it turned out many times, while trying to avoid the standard method of doing something, I'd engage in finding a short-cut, and that usually ended up being the hard way.

This attitude was a daily problem that showed up before grade one and continued all through school, but I carried on, because it had become my 'religion' and though it hadn't worked yet, I was convinced it would. I could never see the big picture; I just focused on what was directly in front of me. Talk about thinking 'inside the box'!

In the early 1950's times were quite different and particularly in parenting style. Most mothers didn't work outside the house and they welcomed the idea of letting the kids go out and play somewhere for most of the day. I had great adventures at the creek and other dangerous areas that no modern parent would allow a 5-year-old to be near while unsupervised. Before I was old enough to start school in grade one, I saw kids riding two-wheel bicycles, which were way faster than the little three-wheeler I had, and if they could do it, so could I — how hard could it be? I found that there was a wonderful selection of bicycles at the school nearby and that's when I realized it was a perfect opportunity for me to learn to ride a real bike. I would go to the school after the bell got all the kids inside the building and pick out the smallest bike I could find, and start trying to get as far as I could before falling. Soon I was able to cruise all over the place, but knew I had to get the bike back before the bell rang and the kids got out.

By the time I was six, I was constantly begging dad to buy me a two-wheeled bike, and he finally agreed to look at the possibility. Of course in those days it was much more difficult to buy used items. It was the newspaper only and there were no pictures or online maps. But dad was a genuinely kind person and though money was always tight, as a retail clerk, he felt he just had to get me a bike. I still remember how excited I was to go in the car with him to look at getting my first bike. It was much too big for me. If I sat on the seat, I couldn't reach the pedals, but it was a "girls" bike, so I knew I could ride it standing up. Dad was ready to pass on this deal and look for something more suitable but I wanted a bike now! I talked him into buying it by telling him I would grow into it. Dad was going to put it into the trunk to get it home where he planned to teach me to ride, and he was very surprised when I said I'd like to ride it home. He couldn't believe I somehow already knew how to ride a two-wheeler. He agreed and drove the car slowly beside me all the way home. I think he just assumed I was unusually coordinated!

My bike and I were inseparable from that point on, as I peddled to the community pool about a mile from home nearly every day in the hot, dry summer school holidays that flitted by over the next few years.

I've always had a short attention span and was continually looking for action, so sitting in a classroom, as a kid was torture. This coupled with the difficulties of Dyslexia, which was virtually unknown back then, made me susceptible to almost any disruption in the normal class routine, in fact if there wasn't some kind of disruption that would draw my attention, I caused one.

Although I did poorly in school, rather than having me repeat a year in the same grade, I was passed on to the next grade because I kept getting the same comments "He can do the work, he just needs to apply himself". As I approached my early teens, I found that girls were becoming more of a distraction attraction in school, even more than all the other fun things that were completely occupying my mind throughout each class.

So when I final got squeezed through grade 8 it was now time to look at High School!

Mom and Dad were well aware of the difficulties I had in school so they decided the discipline of a Jesuit boarding school might be the solution to my problems.

I showed up the first day at Campion College along with enough other students to form three separate grade 9 classes, along with several classes of grades 10, 11 and 12. The three grade 9 classes were sorted according to the performance of each student in their earlier school years. The 'smart kids' were all in the "A" class; the next best were in the "B" class, and of course I landed in the "C" division with the other dumb kids. That's when I noticed it was an all boys school! What a sausage fest!

In that environment one learns how a 'pecking order' develops and the meaning of 'Alpha Male'. I was physically on the smaller side, but naturally muscular, quite athletic and not easily intimidated, so I had no trouble settling into the upper end of the 'peckers' order, and I knew instinctively that a baby face kid with peach fuzz could not be the Alpha Male amongst the big dumb guys in my class that had already started shaving. This experience would come in handy for anyone considering a career in the military.

I squeezed through grade 10, like I had done all the other years in the past, and rather than fail me, since the teachers always knew I was fairly smart, I was kicked forward.

 I transferred to Miller High for grade eleven where I could finally go to school with girls again. Well, that distraction was not helpful and after several behavioral "incidents," I got expelled just before Christmas. Mom and Dad had always been challenged by my endless antics but now they were very concerned for my future. Somehow they got the school to allow me to come back and simply write the final exams. Now that was really showing me that I could get to the end goal without even attending! However they stipulated that I would not be eligible for all the grade eleven credits. I misunderstood that to mean that I would not be eligible to move forward to grade twelve. Unfortunately I didn't appreciate that they were giving me the opportunity to get credits that would count toward a complete grade, so when I took the exams, I exposed my sense of humor by writing joke answers to most of the questions.

So there I was, 17 years old with only grade ten completed, few prospects, and working as a restaurant busboy. It was now early summer of 1967 and we were heading into another long dry summer, but now I had my first car, a 1952 Studebaker Champion with suicide doors that I had bought for $36.00. One inspired, hot, sunny day, the idea of having a convertible became irresistible. So I hacksawed the roof off my car by cutting from the doors to the top of the windshield, hacked the doorposts off flush and then cut from the back doors at the window to the bottom of the back window. There it was: a fresh new "convert"!

The first place I went to show off my new toy was Marcia's house. I pulled up in front and started honking the horn. The first person to come out to see what the commotion was about was her dad! He was not impressed. When Marcia came out, I said, "Come on, let's go for a ride". As she approached, her dad warned her to be careful because he could see the jagged edges. Well, as Marcia got in, she tore her uniform school dress on the shortened doorpost, but she was only one of many to 'catch an edge'.

It was so much fun parading around in my 'convert' but there was another lesson on the horizon. Cars are built with a main frame that runs along the lower internal sides which provides strength and rigidity, and stops the car from twisting or bending. What is not commonly known is that the car roof, which spanning a third of the car's length, acts as a type of truss, which adds significant support to the main frame. Four-door cars like rely even more on the roof for mid-frame stability. Convertible cars do not have the roof truss effect, so they are built with a much larger and stronger main frame. It wasn't long before I noticed that the doors on my new 'convert' were getting 'sticky' and harder to open and close. Within a few weeks the frame had sagged enough that the doors got jammed and never opened again! The 'work-around' on that problem was; to get in, you either jump or climb. But I was young and agile, and so were my friends, so no problem.

I had a great summer with that unique car. I had a tarp that covered the interior at night, and it didn't rain often. If you got caught in the rain, as long as you were moving, the air flowing over the windshield would keep you dry; not so much if I had someone in the back seat. I sold the car before winter set in for $50.00. This proved to me that even if I spontaneously cut the roof off my car, I could be unique, have fun and make money doing it.

I didn't work much that summer so my career was beginning to resemble my school history and the prospects were not good. Mom, who never seemed to get discouraged while trying to help me, kept cutting out job opportunities from the paper, which I had no interest in pursuing. One day however, attached to one of her clippings was an ad to join the army. For reasons I still don't understand, I went down to the recruiting office.

There was a part of me that recognized that Dennis needed something more than me to focus on in his life. He was frustrated with his parents who were trying to get him to get a job or do better at school. He talked about running away, cutting off all ties and showing up at their door when he was old (30) to see if they would recognize him. I tried to talk him out of that.

I think at that point, I became another parental figure that was trying to get him to do the right thing. He became very restless and so it was that in the summer of 1967, Dennis joined the navy. I was stunned. We had just started our romance and he was already leaving. I cried, which my brothers thought was ridiculous and overreacting. They teased me about him going to Vietnam. I cried again. None of us actually knew how bad that would have been. In Canada, we were somewhat protected from the worst parts of that terrible time in history. At any rate, Dennis left for Calgary.

Saved by the Army:

I walked into the small, barren recruiting office with about as much forethought on how this might affect my future as I had on every other decision I had made so far in my life: none. There was a brief and simple questionnaire and an eye test. I failed the eye test because I was nearly blind in one eye from childhood. I had a condition called amblyopia where from birth the brain makes one eye dominant. The cure is putting a patch over the dominant or "good eye" forcing the brain to use the "bad" eye," but if this condition is not detected and properly corrected by age 6, the bad eye will atrophy and never be functional. Unfortunately I didn't get the correct treatment in time. In fact as a kid, when mom and dad found that I couldn't see properly with my right eye, they took me to an eye doctor who gave me glasses with a strong lens for the bad eye! This of course did nothing, or may have even exacerbated the situation because my brain preferred using the "good eye" anyway, so it totally shut down any effort to look through the thick lens, and, as my brain always tended to do, took the "easy way."

The sergeant at the recruiting office said I would have to get glasses in order to sign up for the army. I knew it wouldn't help, but I did it anyway. I came back about a week later to take the eye test again. He was shocked to find that I had just got new glasses and there was no improvement in my vision!

He said, "I like your spunk kid and you're now in the army!" In a few days I was off to boot camp in Calgary.

In Calgary I found myself surrounded by all kinds of guys from all over Canada and most were self professed experts in one thing or the other. On day two, a kid who looked like he was already use to shaving said "Hey you're crazy to be in the army, why not go Navy where you will sail on ships and see the world."

Just a few days after he left, he showed up at the cottage at Regina Beach and we had one or two more days together before he headed out to Nova Scotia, clear over on the other side of the country! Having made this important decision for himself, he had already grown up a bit and was determined to go forward with the plan. I admired him and loved him even more. Diane Renee was singing "Navy Blue" on the radio and I knew just how she felt.

That seemed like good advice to me, so I applied to transfer to the navy and the next day was on a train heading for the navel boot camp in Cornwallis, Nova Scotia.

Somehow, on the way, I managed to get off the train for a day in Regina and again in Montreal. The stop in Montreal was to see my sister Dianne, who is two years older than me, and had left home only months before. She had been in many high school plays where she demonstrated amazing acting ability; so much so, that when the National Theater School in Montreal went across Canada doing auditions, they recruited her. It was nice that I was able to spend a day with her at Expo in Montreal on my way to the east coast.

The bus dumped me off at the main gate of Cornwallis, along with about 35 other scruffy teenagers that had been collected from across Canada. We were marched to our new home for the next few months, an H-style World-War II Quonset hut. Shortly thereafter we were all issued a complete set of new uniform clothes and we each got our head sheared.

From this group of mostly misfit kids thrown together under one roof, a "pecking order" quickly developed. I was one of the smaller guys, but was naturally athletic, unusually strong and not intimidated by unfamiliar situations, so I found myself in the upper portion of that "order." For those near the bottom, life was not fun.

There were about 5 groups like ours going through the 4-month basic training program; each had started a few weeks apart. The "senior" guys were obvious because their blue shirts where more faded, so you could tell who had been there the longest.

In an effort to take the shortcut to seniority, I embarked upon what I thought was a brilliant effort to advance my look to a more seasoned recruit. I put all my shirts in the sink with some bleach and left them overnight.

The next morning I was surprised to find all my shirts were now white with faded blue stitching! I had no other option but to throw one in the dryer, put it on, and go straight out to the parade square where we spent the first part of each day. I was noticed rather quickly as the only white shirt in a sea of blue.

The drill sergeant quickly stormed to within an inch of my face and said, "What's this"? I said, "I accidentally put too much bleach in the wash and ruined all my shirts."

He said, "Get new ones by tomorrow."

To me this meant not only buying new shirts, but also spending most of the night sewing my name on them, so my frugal bones and inventive mind intervened again. I thought I could just dye them back to the right color! So I went to the base "canteen" where they sold most of the basics, however there was no dye that I could find to match, so I mixed what they had available, royal blue and black.

The next morning I found all my shirts in a new shade of bluish grey! Again with no other option I wore one out to the parade square and tried to blend in.

I soon noticed the sergeant marching quickly toward us and sure enough he came straight up to my face again! He looked really mad and I suspected it was my new shirt color that had ticked him off.

He said, "Put your rifle down. Step forward. Left turn. Quick march." He followed behind me directing me toward a building near the main gate. I thought he might be taking me to the stores building where I would get new replacement shirts, but as it turned out he marched me straight to the base jail, where I spent the next two weeks for disobeying a direct order.

It was pretty tough in a military jail. I was alone in a 6 x 8 foot wooden room with a heavy chain-link ceiling and a 6 x 10 inch window facing the hall. The worst part was knowing that no one on the outside knew I was there. They wouldn't let me talk to anyone and they took away all things that could be used to hang yourself, like my belt, shoelaces and even my cap tally, which is the ribbon on your hat. It was very depressing and I wondered how many recruits they lost before they took steps to prevent suicide.

They also took the mattress out of the cell, leaving a bare wooden shelf all day, and the mattress was returned at 8:00PM. They let me out to walk or run around the parade square once a day after dinner. I've never looked forward to running in sea boots without laces since then. I never saw my original division again either. Upon my release from jail I was marched to the stores building to purchase new shirts, then dropped into a newly arrived division where my shirts looked even newer than theirs!

This was another short cut that didn't work as planned, and just the beginning of many more disciplinary issues in the navy on my long road to maturity. I guess in this case I deserved jail time for my stupidity, but unfortunately it wouldn't be the last time I ended up in a military jail!

Target Shooting

In boot camp we had to do a lot of firearms training, which included the FN semiautomatic rifle, 9mm semiautomatic pistol and the Sten gun, a fully automatic 9mm handheld machine gun. I always had trouble with the rifles because they are designed, especially semi-automatic ones, to be shot from your right shoulder. My right eye was so bad I couldn't use it to aim so I had to shoot left-handed, which meant the shells ejected right in front of my face, but I made it work. I liked the machine gun training, as most young guys would. The magazine held 32 rounds and when fired the gun kicked up and to the left. This gun was never designed to shoot accurately; in fact, because of the kicking you shoot this one from your hip. The idea was to use your middle finger on the trigger and point where you want to shoot with your index finger. We were instructed to shoot small bursts on the ground to see where the shots were actually going, and slowly move up to the target. The target was a cardboard figure of a GI in a forward rushing pose. It was about 5 feet tall by about 18 inches wide supported by a 1" x 4" wooden picket planted in the ground.

We each had 3 full magazines to see how many hits we could make on the target, and of course that's what all of the other guys were trying to do, but I wanted to be different. I'm sure the instructors had seen lots of good marksmen over the years that put
a high number of shots in the center of the target, but I thought if I hit the wooden 1" x 4" at the base of the target enough times, I'd be the only guy to have the target fall over! That was my goal, but it turned out to be a much harder task than I foresaw. After nearly 100 rounds focused on a 4-inch wide piece of wood at the ground, my target stayed upright! To say I was very disappointed is an understatement, but maybe the worst part was that because I hadn't hit the real target once; it was embarrassing, because both the instructors noted that they had never seen such a poor shot in their entire careers!

Karma, Sort Of:

One day our class of about twenty guys was at the pool learning various water survival techniques and drown-proof swimming, which has since been discarded, because it is more humane to die quickly of drowning than to drag out your inevitable death due to hypothermia.

We were gathered in a huddle near the edge of the pool watching the instructor in the water below us demonstrate various maneuvers. I was near the back of the pack and quite bored with this very basic instruction, because I had spent nearly every summer day since I was eight years old at the pool in Regina. I was probably more comfortable in the water than the instructor, and thought I could be better than him, but he probably went through a lot of work to get here, and I wasn't prepared to make that effort.

I thought this was a good time to add a little fun to the class, so I reached forward from behind, to the back of one of the guys who seemed to be paying close attention and gave him a little push into the pool. As it turned out, the kid was a poor swimmer and panicked; he took a mouthful of water and nearly took the instructor down! I guess avoiding that kind of thing was the purpose of this class in the first place. To my surprise I found there were lots of guys in the navy who couldn't swim! The instructor in the water couldn't have seen who pushed him in, so I pretended to be as innocent as all the other guys. What I hadn't noticed is that a second instructor had come up to the group from the rear and had a perfect view of me committing the act of class disruption. He grabbed me by the back of my neck and pulled me out of the group and said, "OK wise guy, come with me." He steered me by my neck over to the ladder of the 5 meter high diving board and said, "Get up there, and you're going to stay there until you do a one-and-a- half into the pool!"

I slowly climbed the ladder and tentatively stood at the top on the springboard with a very scared look on my face. But what nobody there knew were the hundreds of hours I'd spent practicing my springboard diving as a kid! He had just ordered me to do one of my easier dives, so I fussed around a bit until he said, "You're not leaving this building until you do it so get on with it." I solemnly nodded then straightened up, strode forward three steps, leaped onto the end of the board, sprung seven feet into the air with toes pointed in a full pike position, completed my turns before passing the board and pulled off one of my best dives ever, including a nearly splashless entry worthy of an Olympic performance. When I came up, everyone was cheering and clapping, even the instructors!

Dennis cliff diving at age 52

When Dennis started boot camp near Halifax, we began to correspond by mail. I still have those letters too. He was very homesick at first and wanted to quit and come home. As much as I wanted that, I somehow knew, even at 15, that he would be better off staying in and building a life for himself. I had a definite feeling that coming back to Regina would lead him in the wrong direction. It was hard on him as he thought that we should get married and then he would have someone with him in Halifax. I was not ready.

When I think back on it, I think we both knew that would not have been the right thing. Dennis was transferred to Victoria and the next few years were turmoil for us, and sometimes we were totally ignoring each other while our lives went on separately. Again, it was a good thing looking back. We both had some growing up to do and as they always say, if it is meant to be, it will be.

Transportation Troubles

After finally graduating from Basic Training, to which my shortcut efforts had added an extra month, I got drafted to CFB Naden, the Canadian Forces (Naval) Base in Esquimalt, British Columbia. I remember the long train ride across Canada, but I was able to arrange a stop in Regina for a few days on my way, where I got a chance to see my friends, Marcia, and Mom and Dad. As a teenager with plenty of discipline problems my relationship with Mom and Dad had been strained, and I still don't understand how they survived all my childhood antics. My mother had a very special gift for communicating. She loved talking with our school friends when they were at our house. In fact we found out later that even after both Dianne and I left home, our friends would come over to visit Mom regularly. When your friends go to see your mother when you aren't there, it tells you a bit about what a special person she is! So every time I had a chance to stop at home while traveling, I never missed an opportunity.

When I finally arrived in Victoria, I thought there must be a lot of people in the rest of the world that have no idea how beautiful this place is. I had a great time just wandering around looking at the natural beauty of the rocky hills and surrounding ocean. Only a few weeks after arriving in

Victoria, I saw an ad on the bulletin board in the barracks saying a guy was being drafted to Halifax and wanted to sell his 4-year-old Honda 450 motorcycle. I had never driven a motorcycle, but how hard could it be? I remember the day I bought that speed machine; how scary it was just holding on when you twisted that throttle.

Ironically, a few months later, I got drafted to Halifax for engineering training. I wanted to keep my bike, so continuing with my kind of forethought, I negotiated a financial arrangement where instead of taking the train, which was paid by the Navy, I would get paid to make my own way to Halifax by the start date of the course. I planned to ride my motorcycle all the way across Canada, stopping in Regina for a few days, have fun on the way and get paid for it! I was very impressed with my negotiating skills.

I learned however, that riding very long distances on a bike designed for speed was extremely uncomfortable and also that heavy rain in the mountain passes leaves you no options but to carry on. On day two of my trek east, after hours of going through a monsoon, I finally arrived at a truck stop. I was so soaked and beat up that when I walked in, the entire place went silent. A trucker took pity on me and asked if I would like a ride to Calgary? We loaded the bike behind his cab and I was very thankful for a chance to dry out and recuperate.

I was getting more serious about my relationship with Marcia, but by the time I arrived at Mom and Dad's house in Regina, my efforts to impress Marcia were somewhat diminished by the two black eyes I had sustained from the rain that had pounded my sunglasses in the mountains.

Based on the first part of this motorcycle journey, I was not really looking forward to the rest of my plan to ride to Halifax. As it turned out, those plans quickly changed while I was goofing around with my buddies. They were in a car and I was on the bike, showing how fast I could accelerate away from them when my leg hit a parked car. I got flipped off the bike and badly injured my lower leg. I needed stitches, but thought a shortcut would do, so I got the doctor to just use a butterfly bandage. I later wished I had gotten stitches because the wound caused ongoing problems later. While in Regina, I put the bike up for sale, bought a train ticket to Halifax and started my engineering career on crutches.

Victoria

After engineering training I got drafted from Halifax to a destroyer back in Victoria, where I lived aboard for several months. I needed to buy a car but didn't have enough cash. I had some money saved and had pawned my nice tape recorder, but was still short so I called my dad in Regina and asked if he would lend me $200.00. He was always ready to give me a chance to show my character, so we agreed on a repayment schedule and he sent a check. I found an Austin Mini for sale and the check arrived on Friday afternoon. I cashed it that day and immediately went over the next morning to buy the car. I was happy to tell everyone about my new ride. Unfortunately one of the guys in our mess on the ship had some money stolen from his locker. When the military police arrived on board, they asked if anyone had been seen with cash or had made any large purchases. I was the only guy who fit that category, so when I returned to the ship Saturday afternoon, they were anxious to talk to me. They asked how I had acquired the money to purchase the car and exactly the denominations I had used in the transaction. When they looked in my locker, they found the pawn ticket. When I told them it was for my tape recorder, they immediately put me in handcuffs and marched me off the ship into the back of the paddy wagon and drove straight to the base jail. I had no idea what was going on or what was happening, but there I was back in a military jail! It was late Sunday when they finally decided to tell me the details. The locker theft had been $200.00 all in twenty-dollar bills and a tape recorder as well as some jewelry intended for the guy's girlfriend. The bank had cashed my check in all twenties, and I had pawned my tape recorder! It certainly looked bad, but I knew the facts would vindicate me; however they couldn't check anything until Monday. Finally late Monday afternoon, they came to my cell and told me they had received confirmation from the bank that I had cashed the check, and received all twenties. They had also taken the guy to the pawnshop to identify the tape recorder, which he confirmed was not his. They even contacted a girl I was seeing at the time to ask if I had given her any jewelry, and that didn't pan out either. They were very disappointed to find that they had the wrong guy, and without even an apology, let me out and drove me back to the ship. The guy who had the gear stolen kind of knew I wouldn't do that, but it did look bad at first, then some months later another guy was caught stealing and they found evidence from the first theft. He was convicted and kicked out of the military.

I had to park my car outside the main gate then walk a quarter mile to the ship so I soon got tired of trying to find a parking spot close to the gate, and that long trek to the ship. So my best friend Barney and I rented a sort-of furnished apartment.

Marcia and three of her friends were planning a driving trip from Regina down through the USA including San Diego and returning via Victoria. I was very excited about that and really looked forward to her arrival.

Finally after what seemed like months of waiting, Marcia showed up and to my surprise had a real California surfboard tied to the roof of her car! I had never surfed, but I was sure going to do it, after all, how hard could it be?

Some months after that visit, Marcia decided to come back out to the coast from Regina, only this time with my sister Margo who was moving to Vancouver. Margo was a real go-getter. She was a teenager moving to the coast to pursue a career in acting and soon landed a job as an on-air host of a kid's afternoon TV show, which lead to co-starring in a European TV series as well as parts in movies like The Great Gatsby and Meatballs.

Marcia was living with Margo in Vancouver and after I made a few visits to see them, I convinced Marcia to move over to Victoria with me.

It had been clear to me for a long time that Marcia was the only person I would marry, so I decided to get her a ring. I put the little ring box in a slightly bigger box and that box in a slightly larger box and so on until I had a nearly one cubic foot package. At half time while we were watching the Grey Cup on TV, I gave it to her.

In the fall of 1969, Dennis and I saw each other at a dance at the University of Regina. It was love at first sight all over again (apologies to Yogi Berra). We began our real relationship then. He was stationed in Victoria and I found a way to visit him out there, and eventually he asked me to marry him.

I had been living with him for a couple of months and we had decided I had to go back to Regina. I actually started to picture my life without Dennis and I was a little excited about maybe going to University. I don't know if that worried him, but just before I left, he gave me a Christmas gift. I thought I would take it with me to Regina to open it on Christmas Day. (It looked like a box with slippers or something in it and I was not that interested in it). He convinced me to open it before I left. The shoebox held a smaller box, and a smaller box until there was a ring box. It was an engagement ring. I said yes.

I went back to Regina to wait until April when we planned to be married. I was working for my Grandmother at the time. She had been injured in a traffic accident and could not do her regular housekeeping chores — which included laundry, changing beds, dusting, washing floors, and making meals for Grandpa and herself.

Chinese Takedown

Marcia and I lived together for a few months and then she decided to go back to Regina to get things organized for our upcoming wedding there. I arrived a month or so later for our life-changing event.

As it turned out there was another nearly life-changing event that occurred just before our wedding. Marcia and I were out one evening and thought we'd stop for some Chinese take-out. The China Bowl, a very small restaurant located across the street from the Grey Nuns Hospital, had been around since I was a kid. The entire building was nothing more than a kitchen with a small bar in front for pay and pick-up. We went in, stood beside another couple and placed our order.

With four people standing at the bar, it was already getting somewhat crowded, then three guys came in behind us. They had obviously been drinking, and one of them was very loud and started swearing. His belligerent behavior continued and was making everyone very uncomfortable, even the hard working cooks. Finally I turned around and asked him to please stop swearing and turned back facing the bar. He completely ignored me and carried on swearing even louder. I realized then that I had not thought this through and put myself in a quandary, which had only one remedy. I knew he had two friends with him so I had to make sure if this developed into something physical outside I wouldn't be so badly outnumbered. So I turned, told him that I had warned him, and punched him in the mouth. He appeared quite stunned and didn't fight back, but I kept hitting him because I knew that I had to put him down for the duration in order to increase my odds with the other two. Marcia seemed as surprised by my action as the guy going down. She was yelling and trying to stop me from continuing to hit him. Then we saw blood coming from the back of his head!

He had been standing behind me directly in front of the windows and my first punch knocked his head back against the wooden window frame which split the back of his head open. There was a lot of blood and when we saw the gash, Marcia suddenly transformed into an emergency care worker. She said, "He needs stitches and I'll walk him over to the hospital"! Right then I realized how fortunate it was that he hadn't been standing just inches to one side or the other, where his head could have gone through the glass resulting in life-threatening injuries. So far I was glad I had avoided being involved
in an "assault causing death" legal action, but now Marcia was volunteering to assist him to the hospital, where I figured I might get the charge reduced to simple assault.

His two buddies seemed satisfied that this incident did not need to continue outside; in fact they said he kind of deserved it! So I asked them to walk him to the hospital and they agreed. Even then, Marcia wanted to accompany them, but I was quite anxious to escape and that was when we heard, "your order ready" so I paid, they left and so did we.

Our First Digs

In preparation for being married, I had rented a small upstairs apartment in Victoria, before going to Regina for our wedding on April 3, 1971. I went to several auctions and got the entire place furnished for about $200.00. Marcia's dad gave us $500.00 and lent us a car to go on our honeymoon in Banff, Alberta, where we had a few days of sightseeing, nice meals and a little shopping. We each used this opportunity to buy something personal that was more expensive than we could normally rationalize. I bought a pair of very stylish "Snoot Boots" which looked like a crossover between a cowboy boot and a Civil War Cavalry issue. They were really unique with nearly knee-high thick leather, steel shanks and attached leather spur straps around the ankle. As it turned out, those steel shanks would be severely tested in the near future.

One day we went for lunch at a hotel at the base of Mt. Norquay. That was the first time we had ever seen a ski mountain. It was very interesting to watch the skiers coming down the moguls. Little did we know that years later skiing would play such a large part in our lives.

Dennis came home just a week before the wedding, which was a small event with no dance because it was Palm Sunday weekend. That suited me fine since I was anxious to be with Dennis, not a bunch of relatives. We had a reception at the Hotel Saskatchewan, and left late afternoon for our honeymoon. My Dad had given us a car to use and $500 dollars to spend. We were already pretty careful of how we spent our money and had a modest holiday in Banff before returning to Regina to drop off the car and then flew to Victoria.

Dennis had rented a small apartment and furnished it with used furniture. It was perfect.

When we got back to Victoria I was so excited to show Marcia our new home, all ready to start living as a married couple! The only downside was that the landlord lived on the first floor and had about a dozen cats. On our first day we came into the vestibule, closed the door and turned the corner to go up the stairs; that's when we came face to face with the "cat herd"! We were halfway up; they were all over the top four stairs. We froze as they got set to attack. Without warning they all jumped, right past us and ran down to the vestibule where they planned to escape, but found the door closed. They all began to jump up on the door trying to get out. Neither of us was prepared to get between them and the door to let them out, so we just started yelling until the landlord came out and saved us. From that point on, we never closed the vestibule door until we checked the staircase first.

I had brought a few of our wedding gifts in my suitcase, so I added new towels, sheets and tea towels to our new home. I was anxious to add to Dennis' efforts to make this little apartment more of a home. I built a bookcase out of two pieces of wood and some concrete blocks — 1970's chic! The landlord saw me carry the bricks from my car and as soon as I had completed the project came to the door and told me that the bricks were too heavy for the floor. I took them back to the lumberyard and replaced the bricks with wine jugs filled with colored water — also very trendy at the time. Finally, a month later, our wedding gifts arrived. The delivery service dropped off a huge box in the vestibule of the building and would not bring it up the stairs to our apartment. I unloaded the gifts in the downstairs hall and carried each item up separately. We had lived without these things for a month and I realized how unimportant "things" were. That would stay with me.

Dennis was stationed on the ship and had to spend every fourth night on the ship.

On top of that, the ship was at sea quite a bit during the first year of our marriage. Dennis had introduced me to a couple on the ship and I spent time with Doreen and her three boys. I also had a part time job at the Clog Box, a local shoe store in downtown Victoria. It was quite a change for me, coming from a large busy family home, to spending a lot of time alone.

On Dennis' 21st birthday, I planned a small party for him and me. I bought a bottle of champagne and made a small birthday cake, which I decorated. I know Dennis would not be home until after 6 that evening. He was under punishment for a problem he had created while taking on water, and instead of coming home at four, he had to work an extra two hours. I waited anxiously but he did not come home. Finally at about 8 o'clock one of his friends phoned to say that he would be staying on the ship that night because he had passed out from drinking too much. I had no idea that the rest of the crew had shared their rum with him that day and he had ended up with more rum than any human should drink.

Of course I was upset, mad and disappointed. Doreen phoned to tell me that the situation on the boat was serious because Dennis had missed muster — showing up for duty at an appointed time — and was going to be charged. Dennis called later to apologize but I was not ready to forgive him. I felt a little sorry for him, but more sorry for myself and cried myself to sleep that night.

Lucky for me and maybe even luckier for Dennis, I woke up the next morning and was not angry, but once again anxious for him to come home. The champagne was still chilled, the cake was fine and we could celebrate that day instead! He came home at six, hung-over, and very grateful that I was not still mad. The celebration was a bit low-key, but this was an important event for our relationship. I forgave easily and wanted things to be peaceful rather than confrontational. This came from within and it was not difficult for me to let go of things.

Motorcycles

It was a year or so since the accident on my Honda motorcycle in Regina so now I had a beautiful Triumph 650cc Bonneville motorcycle with high handlebars that looked great but they were very uncomfortable. If you rode for a long time, the blood would drain out of your arms and it was painful, also you could put your left arm down and shake the blood back in, but you couldn't let go of the right hand throttle or you would very quickly decelerate. As was the case with most English cars and motorcycles, the bike was quite unreliable and it soon became clear that I couldn't continue to strand Marcia at home when I took the car to work because the bike was broken again. I had a two-door Ford Falcon Sedan Delivery that I had turned into a rather nice shagging wagon, so I thought it might be time to get a new motorcycle!

A brand new 650 Yamaha did the trick. But I guess I had forgotten some of the potential downsides of travelling long distances on a motorcycle, so we planned a visit back to Regina on the new bike. To say I planned a bike trip would be wrong, why take the time to figure things out? How hard could it be with two people on a bike? Let's just go; and we just went!

It wasn't even broken in by the time we left with a tent and sleeping bags tied to the sissy bar. On our second day I left Marcia at the campsite near Ferny BC so I could go get gas. This was the first time I had an opportunity to see how fast it would go, so I laid flat on the tank and quickly got it up to nearly 100mph. But very quickly I felt a slight wobble developing from what I thought might be the wind on the sissy bar, so I began to decelerate, however as the speed decreased the wobble dramatically increased! It only took a few seconds to get down to about 60 mph but by then the handlebars were nearly slapping each side of the gas tank. I guess that's why they call this incident a "tank slapper"! As one slows down the back-and-forth wobble takes bigger bites, and the only proper corrective action is counter-intuitive, which is to speed up! That is definitely not your first reaction when this unexpectedly happens at highway speed.

The pickup truck I had just passed at 100MPH was now right behind me at 60 when I hit the pavement! I remember rolling and spinning and seeing the bike skidding with a shower of sparks, but I didn't know where it was in relation to our mutual direction. I hoped it was not behind me because I figured I would stop first and it might skid right over me. Then there was the truck; if I didn't get run over by my bike, would the truck be able to stop in time?

When I finally stopped rolling, the bike went right past me into the ditch, and the truck stopped beside me. A car coming from the other direction stopped as well. These people were so nice. The guy in the car volunteered to go to the campsite and tell Marcia. I told him she could be recognized by her helmet on the picnic table. When he found Marcia and told her I was en route to the hospital, one of the other campers offered to take her there. The guy in the pickup truck took me to the little hospital then went back to pick up the bike and drop it off at the train station, where I had it shipped back to the dealer in BC for reconstruction.

When I limped into the hospital, I was dirty, with matted blood and torn clothes everywhere, and even the steel shank in my snoot boot was broken. The emergency waiting room had chairs all around the walls and the people there looked more like they were waiting for a call from a casting director. It appeared that most people were there just to watch people coming in to the emergency room! I'm sure this offered more excitement than sitting at home or going to a local school baseball game. I needed stitches in several locations including the inside of my mouth. After getting stitched and bandaged, Marcia and I took a bus the rest of the way to Regina.

Surfing

Our first year of marriage was broken into segments of being together at home and me being away at sea. I looked forward to someday getting a shore posting, but was quite excited about an upcoming trip to Hawaii. I got permission to bring that big old surfboard Marcia had bought for me in California before we got married. I could hardly wait to finally try surfing, and on "real waves."

When we tied up in Pearl Harbor, I rented the equivalent of today's SUV, a station wagon, hung the board out the back and headed for the beach. I noticed that Waikiki had little 3-foot waves that may have been OK for novices, and even though I had never surfed, that was just not good enough for me. I had seen surfing contests on TV and that's the kind of wave I wanted to surf.

Why take the time to learn how to surf on little waves; how hard could it be? There must be a shortcut to becoming a world-class surfer! A few inquiries about 'the big stuff' got me to 'the pipeline' at Waimea Bay, where I could expect 15-foot waves. I was surprised to find how far the surfers had to go from shore to catch these monsters. From the beach the dozen or so surfers looked like ants out there. I set the board in the water and started the trek out to the big ones. In only 3 feet of water the first (small) wave hit the board straight on, quickly lifting it right into my face. My nosebleed stopped about the time I finally got out to the surfers.

They were all on much smaller boards with leg lanyards and all were facing out to sea. I didn't have a leg lanyard, which makes sure your board doesn't take off on you after a fall. I also didn't know exactly what they were looking for out to sea, but I did the same as them and planned to do whatever they did. Soon a bunch of them all turned their boards around and started paddling. I found that I had only been able to turn half way around when the wave threw me off and carried on without me. I thought: OK, I'll sit on the board backwards, facing out next time. As soon as they started to turn, I jumped off and back on facing the right way and started paddling. The wave rose beneath me like I was straddled on the top of a fast rising hot air balloon. I started sliding down the front very quickly, realizing, wow! This is not going to be as easy as I thought! I then found that if you don't turn and ride the wave on a diagonal, you come to the bottom of even a 15-foot wave very quickly. While I was in the process of learning this part of surfing the other surfers to my right began to head my way on a collision course. I was on all fours, like a scared dog, and all I could do was hang on. I ran over the back of one surfer's board and we both went flying. I saw my board spinning up in the air about 40 feet away and then disappear. That is when I realized just how small I was in this big ocean. Every few moments between the pounding monster waves, I got a glimpse of the beach about half a mile away. I knew I could not swim that far in these conditions and was beginning to atone for all the other stupid things I had done but gotten away with so far.

Then out of nowhere, the guy I ran over showed up pushing my board with him. I thanked him for my salvation and began paddling straight back. Every time a wave would rise behind and under me, I just bear-hugged the board until it passed and then paddled like hell until the next one came. I was very happy to get that board back to Victoria where it was never used again.

Stealing From the Police

My first trip to San Diego involved several incidents that luckily due to my general ignorance and prolonged immaturity didn't have worse consequences. Of course a day trip to Tijuana Mexico, by simply walking across the border, was high on our agenda. This foreign culture was very new to me. The poverty was shocking, and there were street vendors everywhere, mostly selling the same stuff, like tooled leather purses, belts and sandals with soles made from car tires. They all had novel products, but one that stands out was a small gourd about the size of a large egg that four toothpick legs, two toothpick ears, a toothpick tail and a small cork inserted for a snout on a painted pig face. What made this thing interesting was if you picked it up and set it down, you could hear it buzz and the ears and tail would twitch! It turned out that after you bought it for a dollar, and took it home to see what made it work, by removing the cork, a fly would come out and it never worked again! I could never figure out how they got a live fly in the gourd through that little corked hole.

I also learned a valuable "negotiating" lesson in Tijuana. Every transaction was the result of an extended back and forth negotiation process. Some friends had purchased switchblade knives for about $2.00, and each had started at an asking price of $5.00. I thought I'd like one of those switchblades too, but I'll try a different method of negotiating, a shortcut to speed up the process, so when I went into one of the street shops, I handed the guy $2.00 bucks and said "I want a switchblade knife." He said, "OK," and then he put the money in the cash drawer and showed me a dinky little $2.00 toy knife. I said I want this one, and grabbed the $5.00 knife. He quickly grabbed the knife from my hand and said, "No, for two bucks you get this one," pointing back to the toy. After I recognized I had given him all the negotiating power, and he was not going to capitulate, I asked for my money back. He refused, so I pushed him aside, went to the cash drawer and made a $2.00 withdrawal. I was quite surprised when he immediately flicked open the switchblade in his hand and made a swipe at my throat! Fortunately just as he made the lunge toward me, his co-worker grabbed him from behind to restrain him. That intervention saved my life, because the knife only cut a slight scratch across my throat, though the blood ruined my white uniform gun shirt. That's when I vowed to never try that negotiating premise or remedy again, and I vowed to never go to Mexico again.

I remember really looking forward to sailing to Tonga, Samoa, New Zealand, Tasmania and Australia. I had heard about crossing the equator, where the ship's crew falls into two groups; those that had crossed the equator, called Shellbacks, and those that hadn't, called Tadpoles. Aside from the various bogus stories that abounded, such as water going down a sink drain spins in the opposite direction once you cross the equator, I was surprised at the size and scope of the "Line Crossing Ceremony." On the aft deck of the destroyer a few days before we were scheduled to make the "crossing," they built an elaborate stage and pool filled to about 5 feet deep with seawater.

At the edge of the stage they mounted a chair with fixed hinges on the two back legs. At the time of the crossing, a group of Shellbacks got into costumes and formed into King Neptune's Court, a group of the really big guys were the "bears" waiting in the pool and a round-up squad made up the rest. The round-up guys had a list of everyone on the ship that hadn't shown their shellback card; of course if it was your first time, you didn't have one, and even if you did have one but didn't have it with you on this trip, you were treated as a Tadpole. The Tadpole treatment was as follows:

The round-up guys would search the ship for everyone on the list, and there was nowhere to hide. When they found you, they would take you forcibly to the aft deck where you would be marched up on stage and held in the chair. One of the King's court would plaster your face with shaving cream, making sure your nose was covered, so when you opened your mouth to breathe another "court" enforcer would jam a horrible mix of cayenne pepper and cinnamon powder mixed with bread crumbs in your mouth. Then they would push the chair backwards dumping you head over heels off the hinged chair into the pool where the bears were waiting to dunk you while you tried to spit out the crap in your mouth. It was quite an experience!

Be it known to all that:
AB D.A. PINVIDIC

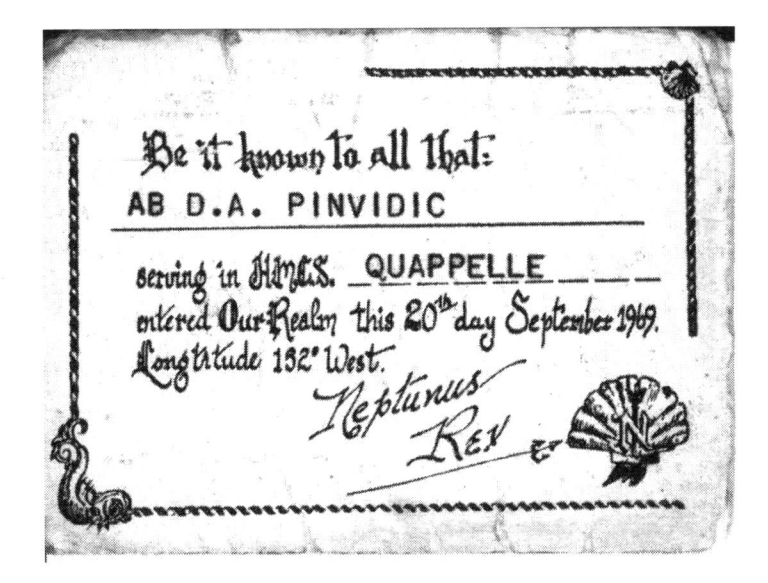

serving in H.M.C.S. QUAPPELLE
entered Our Realm this 20th day September 1969.
Longitude 132° West.
Neptunus Rex

At the time it seemed like the only purpose for our arriving on a navy ship at some foreign port was to over-drink while displaying our sailor uniforms, and get into some kind of trouble. Late one evening in Hawaii on our return from a bar with my core of three friends, just after entering the base, I thought it would be appropriate to bring some memorabilia back to the ship. There was a sprinkler watering a grass section so I went over, disconnected the hose, gathered it up along with the sprinkler head and began carrying it back toward the ship. My buddies couldn't figure why I would want that gear, and nor could I. I guess it's like a dog chasing a car! What is he going to do if he gets it?

I didn't have much time to come up with a reason because without warning the military police came up from behind and swept me into the paddy wagon without saying a word. They took me straight to the main gate where most bases kept their jail cells. I was standing there while they began getting my information when an older Canadian petty officer walked in. He was from the other destroyer that was in Pearl Harbor with us. In a big booming voice he asked, "What's going on here"? Once he saw it was a misdemeanor, he said, "I'll take care of this asshole!" When they turned me over to his custody, he said, "Right turn, quick march." I marched out of the cellblock with him directly behind me. As soon as we were out of their sight, while continuing to march, he asked if I was on the other ship? I said yes, then he said, "Well get the hell there"! He turned to go to his ship and I went straight to mine.

The next stop on our way back to Victoria was San Diego, where the city cops picked four of us up for public intoxication and took us to the city jail. This is where they would gather all the delinquents, bums, booze artists and general troublemakers and usually keep them overnight. We were dumped at the desk of the duty officer where we stood around answering his questions. He decided not to throw four uniformed Canadian Navy sailors into jail with the other reprobates so we hung around his desk while he arranged for the paddy wagon to take us back to our ship.

When we got down to our mess, one of the guys said, "Look what I got off the sergeants desk" as he pulled out a brand new "violation ticket book." I said, "Well, look what I got," as I pulled out a set of handcuffs! Then we heard, "How about this," as the third guy shows us a framed certificate he took from the wall! We had a good laugh at how we had spontaneously done this mischief without uttering a word to each other. About an hour later one of the guys on duty at the gangway came down to the mess to inform us that the cops are on shore asking about some stolen gear. We negotiated a deal where all the loot was returned and there were no further questions or action.

Taking On Water

I had one of the best jobs on a ship an engineer can have, which is being in charge of the water on board. I made sure all tanks were full for sailing, and while underway, I was in charge of the evaporators that made fresh water from the ocean. I also enforced the "Navy Shower" protocol, which was; no shower could exceed 3 minutes from start to finish, a practice I still engage for myself today.

All crew members were required to be onboard at least eight hours prior to sailing, and because on this particular trip we were leaving at 7:00AM, and I had to fill all the water tanks, I decided to stay on the ship rather than go home for dinner and then return to the ship the same evening. I had already "dipped" all of the water tanks, which means using a long metal measuring tape with a weight on the end, sending it down a three foot high "sounding tube" until it hits the tank bottom, then reading the water level on the tape against a chart on the bulkhead. Each tank had a filling valve located at deck level opposite its sounding tube. The water to fill the tanks came through a one and a half inch hose from shore at about 60 PSI and from there was distributed to all of the water tanks on board via pipes and isolating fill valves. Just as the water gets near the top of the tank, which you can only determine by successive dipping, the next tank valve is opened while the current tank valve is slightly turned closed to restrict the flow and allow accurate topping up before fully closing the valve.

At about 10:00PM I started filling the first tank, which was only half empty but still took 20 minutes to fill. I had four more empty tanks, so it was going to be a very boring couple of hours. But I had an idea! A shortcut! After precisely timing the filling operation on two tanks, I determined I could play bridge for 23 minutes with 2 minutes to spare. So I set up filling the third tank and went back to the mess to play bridge for 20 minutes.

I loved to play bridge with a few other guys that knew the game, and because most of the crew was now on board, we started to play in the mess after dinner. At one point one of the guys asked if I was supposed to be taking on water? That's when I realized I'd completely forgotten to pay attention to the time. I looked at my watch and found I'd been playing bridge for 40 minutes!

I ran all the way to the hatch where the fill valve for that tank was and found the hatch closed! This hatch is not usually closed, but when I opened it, I saw why it was closed! The last three rungs of the ladder were underwater, as well as the isolating fill valve, so I couldn't even get down there to shut the water off. Just as I realized I would have to go to shore to shut the supply valve, I heard, " Emergency! Emergency! Flooding in the forward lower deck"! I told the gangway staff I would get it under control as I ran past them to the shore water valve, but it was too late. The young duty officer had been asleep in bed when he heard the emergency broadcast and stepped into about 4 inches of water in his cabin, in fact his shoes had floated away! The tank air vent was located in his cabin and when the water overfilled the tank, it poured through the vent, flooding his cabin. He thought the ship was actually sinking and in a panic called the ship's captain at home!

It took me until about 4:00AM to get all the pumps and lines rigged and evacuate all the water from the flooded spaces. We were still able to sail on time the next day, but I ended up under punishment for two weeks for that lesson on shortcuts.

When To Run?

Standing one in three watches means working one 8-hour shift every 24 hours in the boiler room or engine room. It was very tiring and dangerous; especially after hearing of the disaster on a Canadian destroyer like the one I was on, which occurred while they were doing exercises off the East Coast. There were seven engineers killed when the lubricating oil for the main gearboxes caught fire. The main gearboxes hold nearly 600 gallons of lube oil, with vents located on the upper deck. The upper deck crews that keep the ship looking bright and shiny had been using brass polish on the vent screens, and over time, unknown to the engineers, the vents became clogged. The pressure built up and eventually caused one of the big oil lines to rupture. As a result of the huge leak, the oil pressure in the gearboxes dropped to a dangerously low level so the engineer of the watch hit the emergency button that alerted the bridge, and then called the chief engineer. By the time all the department heads arrived, all the oil had been pumped into the engine room bilge. When it subsequently caught fire, the escape ladders melted, killing everyone in the space. The fireball also flared up through the open engine room hatch into the ship's main passageway. The engine room hatch was usually left open and in this case remained open because in order to close it, one had to reach over the now flaming hatchway to undo the slide lock. One of the bundles of wiring that traveled the length of the ship was located directly over the engine room hatch. So when the polyvinyl chloride (PVC) wire insulation caught fire it gave off chlorine gas. Several others were killed and injured during this horrific tragedy.

There was immediate remedial action taken to modify all the other destroyers in the Canadian fleet. The hinges and slide locks for the engine and boiler room hatches were relocated. Ships were no longer allowed to sail with hatches open. Machinery vents were removed from the upper deck and now vented directly into the machinery spaces, which were required to sail with a negative pressure produced by extraction fans.

Only weeks after we had completed the modifications that were prompted by the accident, it was nearing midnight and I was on watch in the engine room returning from Pearl Harbor. We were slowly rocking from side to side between large rolling waves when the watch engineer walked behind the control console to look at the steam turbines and main gearboxes. He came running back and immediately hit the emergency button and spun both of the big throttle wheels shut! I couldn't hear him explain what he'd seen because when he shut those throttles, 550 psi of superheated steam, which had previously been flowing to the main turbines suddenly had nowhere to go and when the safety relief valves blew in the boiler room it was like a very large bomb went off in the middle of the ship.

He repeated "there's a fire in the starboard gearbox! Grab the flashlight and come with me." We got on top of the gearbox and began looking for flames through the thick glass inspection panels. When I looked up I saw the chief engineer, the engineer officer, the ships executive officer and at least one other department head had already arrived in the engine room. I realized how all those guys died in the east coast accident and started to consider my departure time. After all, the escape ladders were still there! But I sure didn't want to be the first guy to head out. So I thought I'd wait a little longer and hope my timing would work out.

When it was clear there was no fire and no oil leak, we were told to keep the engine shut down and sail the rest of the way on one engine. I was still on the top of the gearbox so the chief told me to "put in the turning gear," which is an electrically driven gear that we engage manually to turn the main gears very slowly after shutdown in order to avoid warping from residual heat.

I tried pulling the turning gear lever, but it just ground the gears. After several unsuccessful, grinding attempts I told the chief it would not engage. He then realized the ship was still drifting through the water and the main propellers were turning, and thus turning the gears. So the chief gave the astern throttle a little kick of steam to try to stop the propeller. I pulled the lever again, but still no joy. He had given it a little too much steam and now the prop was slightly turning in reverse. After several of these back and forth grinding attempts, it finally engaged.

When we got back to our home base in Victoria there was an army of white hats and coveralls waiting for us. Only those with special training and security clearance were allowed to re-enter the engine room once the gearbox was opened for the investigation.

After about 3 weeks there was a report issued which concluded that due to the continued rocking that evening, vapors had been trapped in the corners of the gearbox and at precisely the time when the chief had gone to look, the sea state flattened allowing the accumulated smoky vapors to exit the vent on top of the gear box. The only unexplained condition was the discovery of a large quantity of brass filings in the lube oil.

When I heard about the brass in the oil, I knew it was because of me grinding the gears trying to engage the turning gear. So I went to the chief's mess and asked to speak to him. He came out and when I reminded him about the turning gear incident his face turned white as a sheet. He said, "Did you tell anyone"? I said, "No, it just occurred to me." He looked me straight in the eye and said, "Well, don't!" I guess because this problem no longer involved us, he wanted to keep it that way.

Only a few weeks later he got promoted and I got a shore posting!

Part Two

A Tropical Island?

Our first year of marriage was a period of adjustment for me. I was extremely homesick and Dennis was away for weeks at a time. I cried a lot that first year. Just before our first anniversary, we got a surprise posting to Masset in the Queen Charlotte Islands (now called Haida Gwaii.) We had only a month to prepare for the move. The military paid for the move, including packing and shipping our belongings. We were given a choice of flying or taking a cruise up to the islands. We chose the cruise thinking that it would be a romantic anniversary trip. We didn't do a lot of research and found ourselves on a freighter, in bunk beds, sharing a bathroom with another couple, and travelling slowly through rough seas. I lived on Gravol and spent quite a bit of the trip in bed (alone).

When we arrived in Masset, we were surprised at how small and remote it really was. Food arrived by barge and the grocery store could run out of basics like milk and fruit.

Dennis enjoyed his time there, learning to fish and hunt and take in the activities offered in that part of the world.

We had recently purchased our first brand new car, a 1971 Ford Cortina, when I received orders that I was being transferred. It was a posting to Masset in the Queen Charlotte Islands! We were quite excited, anticipating life on an island in some tropical archipelago but were quickly brought back to earth when we looked up our destination in the encyclopedia.

Masset was a very small Canadian military base on the north island of what is now known as Haida Gwaii, located west of Prince Rupert, BC. I was scheduled to report for duty there on April 4, 1972, the day after our first wedding anniversary.

We had a few choices on how to get there. We could drive all the way to Prince George in the northern interior of BC, then west to Prince Rupert and ship the car over from there, or ship the car from Vancouver by barge and fly there. But I found that the barge that would take our car also offered accommodation for up to 6 people sailing directly from Vancouver to Masset. I thought wouldn't it be nice and romantic to make this our first anniversary cruise! No need to do any further research, this was going to be great!

I was uncomfortable when I saw them lift our new car onto the deck of the barge where it would stay for the three-day trip, and having sailed these waters before in destroyers, I knew it was in for plenty of salt spray. But a few more surprises were waiting when we got aboard and they slipped away from the jetty.

Our "state room" was about 7 feet by 4 feet, just enough room to hold the two bunk beds! There was a "shared head" or bathroom, which we and another unfortunate and equally uninformed couple would share for the next 3 days. We also would share meals and lots of leisure time with the smelly diesel scent of the off duty crewmembers in the 10 x 10 communal lounge / dining room. One thing about travelling like this is that it really made us appreciate arriving at our destination!

My new job would be taking care of the main building heating, air-conditioning, and "no-break" electrical supply system, as well maintain the base swimming pool. These land-based systems were going to be new to me, but the basics still fell within my engineering training, however many new life experiences awaited us there as well.

Masset was a very small, isolated, one street Haida village with only basic amenities that seemed to exist primarily for the military base that was located there. The base was set up mainly for Canadian personnel but had a steady contingent of U.S. military visitors. Its principle purpose was to triangulate the position of all shipping in the Pacific Ocean between Washington State, Hawaii and Alaska. The early, computerized technology was also able to listen to all maritime radio traffic. The base operated under very high security due to the ongoing cold war with Russia. The isolation of this base was a curse and also a blessing as the unpaved logging roads led to many pristine forests, rivers and lakes that surrounded the town. This was heaven for anyone that liked the natural outdoors, and especially if you were into fishing or hunting, neither of which I had ever done.

Most of the people we met there over the next two years truly relished the abundance of outdoor opportunities and had asked for extensions to their postings or left the military in order to stay there.

Outdoor Activities

Shortly after arriving it became clear we would have to get into the common culture of outdoor activities. Fishing seemed to be the easiest and most logical way to get started, and as luck would have it, I saw a full page ad on the back of a magazine that showed a complete 900 piece fishing kit. This 8-by-10 full page ad pictured the entire 900 pieces laid out, which included three collapsible fishing rods with reels, each for a supposedly different type of fishing, as well as three spools of declining weight fishing line, various lures, bobbers, weights, and several boxes of single hooks. All of this 'top of the line' gear could be purchased for the low price of $19.99.

It arrived a few weeks later in a cardboard carton about the size of a breadbox!

After hearing the fishing stories about landing those big ones, I was quite disappointed with the look of this kit. It seemed more suited for a 4-year-old kid.

The heaviest line in the kit was 7 lb. test, about the thickness of a human hair! Well, I bought this kit so I was going to make it work. I figured I would modify it a bit and still be able to use most of the pieces. I went to the local store and purchased 50 lb. test fishing line; no fish was going to break that line!

This fishing line was about the size of house wiring, and when I tried winding it onto the largest one of those little closed faced reels, I could only get about 12 feet on and still be able to get the cover over the reel. I hoped I wouldn't have to cast more than 3 or 4 feet and that the water wouldn't be deep!

My first outing was accompanying a guy and his wife to do some fishing. When I tried casting with my new gear, the line was so thick it wouldn't go through reel guide. After several unsuccessful attempts, I decided to just stick the rod handle in the mud on the bank, pull all the line off the tiny reel and hand toss it into the water. But 12 feet of line just isn't enough to get the hook into deeper water just off the shoreline. So my vision of getting any value from my fishing kit was extinguished quickly. Finally I just pulled about 60 feet off the spool of heavy test line, tied a hook on it and threw it out like I was lassoing a steer. I stood there holding the line with bare hands and tugging like it was on a proper rod. Amazingly, I got a tug back! I yelled, "I got one" and started pulling the line in hand over hand. I pulled the fish into shore and just as this 10-inch trout got on the beach the hook came out of its mouth! It started wiggling and flipping all over the place and I was very concerned that my first fish might slide down the sloped bank back into the water! I wasn't going to let this fish get away, but I certainly wasn't going to touch it with my hands. So I did the only thing I could; I grabbed the thin tip of my fishing rod and started swatting the muddy handle at the fish. Finally, just as it got near the water's edge, I hit it, and the battle was over.

The guy's wife had arrived to see what the commotion was about. After seeing the latter part of this struggle, she knew I didn't have a clue as to what to do next. She offered to help clean the fish. Fortunately I had anticipated the possibility of catching something and brought Marcia's rubber gloves from the kitchen. I put them on and knelt over the fish across from her. She grabbed the fish with her bare hands and began to fillet it right there. Unfortunately her husband came by, and saw me hunched across from her, watching with rubber gloves on but not touching, while his wife had the fish and the knife. He took a picture that circulated through the village and needed no caption!

The deer on the island had no natural predators and were so abundant you couldn't go outdoors for more than 5 minutes without seeing half a dozen. So hunting was very popular. I bought an old British army single shot .303 rifle for $15.00 and asked the best-known hunter on the base to take me out hunting. He had a fancy high power rifle with a scope and was happy to show me the way a real hunter does it. We passed many deer on the way up as we drove to a high point where he liked to look down at the deer in the valley. We were standing beside his car looking down for signs of movement when he said "there's one," and grabbed his gun. He used the front of his car to rest his elbows. Just as I saw the deer he was targeting, I heard the gunshot. It had a very strange sound but I thought that might be the difference between his new hunting rifle and my old war relic. I noticed the deer continue on its way so he had clearly missed. He looked a little embarrassed and confused. I then saw what had caused the unusual sound of the shot, and the reason he missed the deer. He was shooting in a slightly down direction, while resting on the front of his car. He had the deer clearly in the scope, which was mounted about 2 inches above the gun barrel, but his gun barrel did not have the same line. He had shot through the front corner of the hood of his car!

There were lots of good times in that little community. We got involved in all the activities; even playing Bingo at the community center, where one of our highlights occurred when I won three times in one night including the jackpot! We went home with over $200.00 that night, and that was more than half a months' pay. The next day I bought Marcia her first sewing machine. Marcia got so good at creating things on that sewing machine that while I was away for a week in Ontario attending a basketball referee course, compliments of the government, she made me a three-piece suit. There was nothing she couldn't make.

The annual Yakoun River Race was pure, crazy fun. The criteria allowed only handmade vessels, nothing new or purchased, and limited constructed materials to wood, screws and rubber. The island was laden with old fishing and logging relics where I found an old Euclid earthmover tire that had an inner tube in it. A guy I worked with agreed to enter the competition with me, so we cut the inner tube into two equal lengths, closed off each end to make somewhat curved pontoons and tied them to an old piece of plywood. We paddled down the rushing river with about sixty other entrants, each with their own crazy contraptions and accompanying costumes. It was a real spectacle watching ideas clash with reality when the rubber hits the wash. Ours was one of the few that actually performed as planned and we finished in the top three.

An older 35-year-old civilian who I worked with and really liked was a one of the smartest people I've known. He was uneducated, or at least not formally educated — but was a natural engineer. He was into dune buggies and motorcycles. He was also the only motorcycle dealer on the island, the dealer/rep for Kawasaki, a business which he ran from his basement. He was always in the process of building dune buggies, which he had raced several times.

The annual Dune Buggy Race was approximately a half-mile, cross-country trek through wooded trails and up and down sand dunes on the beach. It was open to any and all vehicle classes including motorcycles. It had been over a year since my last motorcycle accident; so I thought it was just about time to get another one. I never had a dirt bike and certainly had never competed, but I thought a new 125 Kawasaki dirt bike would be a great way to get started and entered the race.

On the day of the race, I heard of a trick; lower the pressure in the rear tire to increase grip in the sand dunes, and of course tape up the headlight to avoid damage from flying rocks. In keeping with my philosophy of "if a little is good, more is better," I lowered the air in the back tire until it looked noticeably low. It was three grueling laps. I was very surprised to find that the fatigue that set into my arms was indescribable. I found that I was able to stay near the front but on the last lap, as I jumped over a dune, when I landed the rear tire gripped and the wheel spun slicing the air fill valve off the inner tube. The tire went flat immediately.

Though stability was now a real effort, I was still able to keep up to the kid in the lead, but I just couldn't get past him. Then about 100 yards from the finish line he fell off the bike and was so physically drained, he couldn't pick the bike up. I slowly rode past him with a flat tire to win the trophy for First Place Motorcycle Division! At the finish line I realized how fortunate I was that I hadn't dropped my bike, because I was so spent and exhausted from the race that I couldn't even muster the strength to undo the chinstrap of my helmet.

The Cabin

Experiences over our two years in Masset were numerous and sometimes noteworthy, but none surpassed the saga of a trip to the island just off Port Clements in Masset Inlet. I had heard all about "the cabin" on the island, located a few miles south in the inlet that had been built some 30 years earlier, and was left for anyone that wanted to use it. One day our neighbor, who was the head of the military police, asked if I'd like to go on a weekend hunting/fishing trip to the Cabin. I didn't have to think about it; I was in. He was also in charge of the only boat owned by the military, a 40-foot whaler that had just been put back in the water following an extensive bottom refit. We loaded the boat with food, lots of beer, several guns, sleeping bags, spare gas tanks, extra spark plugs for the outboard, tools and everything else one would need to spend a month or so in the wilderness.

It was a beautiful Friday afternoon in April when our wives waved good-bye from the docks, as we set out for a well-planned and highly anticipated 2-day adventure.

I had never asked how far it was to the island, and was surprised to learn that we were going to be steaming at our full speed of about 5 knots for at least 4 hours, depending on tide action. We had gone through several beers when the thought of shooting empty beer cans from the boat started to look like a good idea. I had my war issue .303 rifle but I also had my 22 cal. semi-automatic rifle which I brought out and began shooting! Well, he was 'the cop' and said, "Hey, look what I brought." He pulled out a couple of handguns! I put the rifle down, completely forgetting about the danger that because it was a semi-automatic, it was cocked and loaded. We spent the next hour or so drinking and shooting. By the time we arrived at the island, we were both quite impaired, but we were anxious to get settled in. He was very clear that we were not to put the boat on the beach because he didn't want to scratch the new bottom paint. So we jumped into about a foot of water while he held the boat and I unloaded the food and supplies that we would need for the night.

He said, "OK, we're going to kedge anchor the boat." He was an air force cop, and I had actually sailed on a ship in the navy, but I didn't have a clue what he had in mind. The idea was to balance the anchor on the front of the bow, shove the boat out into about 10 feet of water, and then give the anchor line a tug, it will fall off the boat, and there it is, securely anchored. With the anchor line in hand he pushed the boat out and when it was about 50 feet away gave the line a shake and just like clockwork, the anchor wobbled and fell off the boat. Wow, I thought this guy is a genius! But to our surprise, the boat just kept floating away. That's when we realized he had forgotten to tie the anchor to the boat!

In April the northern Pacific Ocean water temperature is about 38 degrees Fahrenheit, but there was no choice, someone had to go after that boat! I stripped down to underwear and dove in. By now the boat was a long way away, so by the time I swam to it I was nearing hypothermia. Only when I was in the water looking up at the gunnels of a 40-foot boat did I get the true perspective of how high those sides are. I was in my early 20's, athletic and very physically fit, but it was all I could do to climb up into that boat. Now, impaired, soaking wet in just briefs, a slight breeze was blowing me further away. I was absolutely freezing! I tried pulling the cord on the outboard a couple of times but it wouldn't start, so I grabbed an oar and started paddling. By the time I got the boat to shore, it was clear I was in real distress. I could hardly talk. He pulled the boat onto the beach, threw the anchor into the boat and tied the line to a tree, then helped me get into a sleeping bag and laid me on one of the bunks.

By now it was getting dark. He carried the supplies from the beach and dumped most of the stuff just inside on the floor except for the bread, the gas lantern and a few toiletries, which he put on the table. In the dark I heard him filling the lantern with gas, then light a match. That's when the entire table went up in flames and right in the middle of the fire was the gas can! He looked like he was trying to save the bread, so I sprung out of my near comma, jumped up, grabbed the gas can and threw it as far as I could out the door. I didn't realize there was a cliff there and that was the last we would see of our fuel.

When I turned back he was still trying to get things out of the fire. I pulled the tablecloth half off the table, then folded it back on top and started pounding down on it. The flames were gone and we were now out of danger, however most of our food was a melted mash of organic and plastic materials. Without saying a word, we both got into our sleeping bags and crashed.

The next morning we looked out to see a 6-inch blanket of snow over everything! He prepared to light a fire in the potbelly wood stove in the middle of the cabin, however there was no kindling inside. So he put what small logs were there in the stove and went out to the boat to scavenge through the snow covered supplies and got a quart of outboard motor oil. I saw him pour some of the 2-stroke oil on the stove contents. When he lit a piece of paper on fire and threw it in. That stove came alive! I thought I saw it do a little dance before it landed again, but at least it didn't explode and we had instant heat.

We planned for lots of fishing and hunting adventures, but hadn't contemplated just filling time. One of the few items of food that hadn't been lost in the fire was a box of cereal. So I cut the box into 52 small rectangles and drew card faces on each piece. We played a few games but it was very difficult to hold a hand and nearly impossible to shuffle a deck that stood nearly 6 inches high.

Fishing in the cold was not attractive, but maybe we could hunt. He suggested we take the boat and circle the island looking for deer coming to the water. We dragged the boat, with the new bottom paint back to the water where it had been left high and dry from the high tide, and began to circle the island. Only a few minutes later we saw a deer on the beach that I could have shot from the boat but he turned the boat and headed straight for it. So it hopped into the woods. I asked why he had done that, and he said "Because we can track it in the snow." Again, I thought, what a genius!

We pulled up on shore and began following the tracks into the wilderness. We never saw the deer ahead of us, but after nearly an hour of 'tracking' on this very small island, we came across more fresh tracks, but they were shoe tracks! That's when we realized they were our own footprints! The deer had led us on a big circle and was somewhere in the bushes laughing.

It was nearly noon and the prospects for any more fun were drastically diminished, so when he suggested we head home it was like music to my ears. We loaded the boat and started our 4-plus hour journey back. I was in the front facing back and he was at the stern facing me, looking right into the light snow falling as he steered the outboard. We didn't talk for the entire trip.

As we neared the amphibious airport at the end of town, he pulled out the military police handheld radio and called his on-duty sergeant and asked him to meet us there to unload the gear before we got to the docs. Unloading at the water-taxi airport made things much easier because the sergeant could drive the truck right to the water. He met us there and helped us unload everything from the boat, then went on his way. That was when we learned that someone had loaded the outboard fuel tank, with the tools as well as the oars! All we had was one piece of 2x4 lumber. So rather than making an embarrassing radio call, we splashed forward the last 100 yards to the docks.

Later, after finally getting warm at home I began to see the humor in this outdoor adventure fiasco. I found it to be a pretty funny story, but when it somehow got into the local newspaper, my neighbor the cop didn't want to take on any more adventures.

Our New Arrival

About halfway through our posting I wondered about asking for an extension, but Marcia was quite clear that two years in this isolated location was more than adequate. Then came the news, we were going to have a kid! About six months into the pregnancy it was determined that due to Marcia's signs of gestational diabetes she would have to go to a more capable hospital for the delivery.

We made arrangements for her to go to Regina where both our families lived, and she would have more support. I could fly there just in time for the birth.

Shortly after we arrived in Masset, I became pregnant. The medical facilities were limited, but other women had successfully had their babies there and I was not concerned. For some reason, the doctor decided to test me for diabetes and the test revealed that I had gestational diabetes. Because this involved some risk for the birth, a decision was made to send me away from Masset for the last three months of my pregnancy. The choice was Vancouver, which would have involved a hotel stay, or Regina, which meant I could stay with my parents. Since Regina was a cheaper and more practical move, the military made that choice.

The doctors in Regina re-tested me and informed me that I was not diabetic after all, but that it was a good idea for me to be in Regina instead of Masset. Dennis was still in Masset, scheduled to come on about May 1 just a few days before my due date of May 11. Two weeks before that date, on April 27, Brant arrived without too much difficulty. Dennis arrived two days later. We had not chosen a boy's name — for some reason, we believed it was a girl, who we planned to call Lisa.

When Marcia left for Regina, we were calling the baby "lump" and because he decided to jump out two weeks early, I didn't have a chance to get to Regina in time for the birth, so that remained his name until we settled on Brant a few days later.

For the first two days of his life, Brant was Baby Boy Pinvidic. Dennis found the name Brant in a book and when he arrived, we started to call the baby by that name.

Two weeks after, we flew home to Masset. I loved being a mother and Brant was a wonderful, bright little boy. Dennis and I were on our second year and scheduled to leave around the date of our anniversary. We began the countdown, like so many others who lived up there. We left in early April and took a trip to Regina on our way to Victoria.

Brant was just one year old when I got a posting to take the next level training at the engineering school in Victoria. We took a roundabout trip there from Masset via Regina in a van I had customized into a sort of camper. We rented a small apartment in Esquimalt near the base and looked forward to the next adventures that lie ahead.

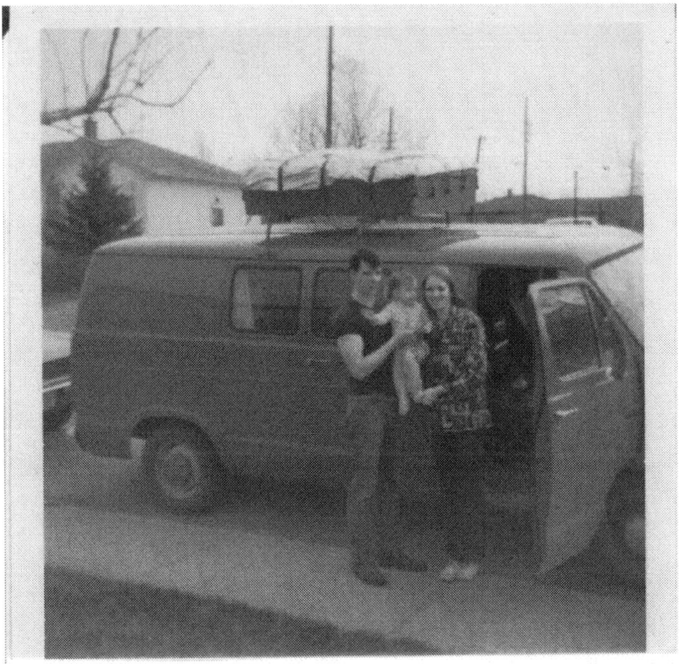

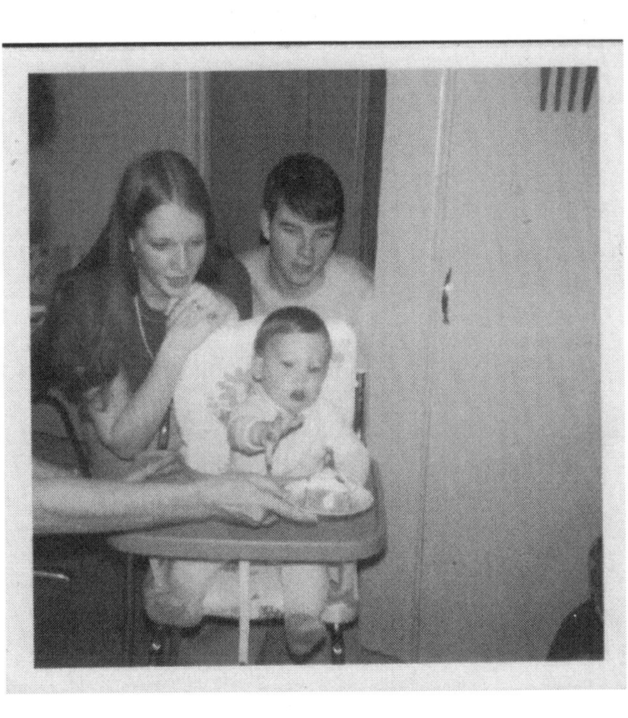

Our Second New Arrival:

We rented an apartment on Sussex Street — just one block over from where we had lived before we went to Masset. We were expecting our second baby, so decided to look for a house. Dennis had started buying and selling cars with his cousin and we had managed to save enough money for a down payment. After a couple of false starts, we bought a house that had been moved to a new foundation and remodeled to be like new. Dennis was back on the ship, and once again we had long separations and overnight duties. My first night in the house was New Years Eve 1975. Dennis was on duty on the ship, so I was alone in the house. Suddenly I heard a bang — like someone hitting a barrel. It stopped and started several times and I was convinced that someone was in the basement, trying to drive me crazy. At the time, I slept with a rifle under the bed, so I loaded it and went downstairs. I heard the noise again, only this time it was clearly outside not in the basement. I tracked it down and found that the temporary address sign wired to our front stairs was banging in the wind against the front stairs — a hollow concrete structure — much like an empty barrel. I was able to lay the sign up on the top of the stairs and finally went to sleep.

I became less comfortable with the rifle under the bed. Brant was growing up and had turned two. He was an active, curious little boy. I had to convince myself that I wouldn't (ironically) need to use the rifle on the first night I did not have it, and then I was fine.

Shawn David was born on July 22, 1975. Dennis was with me this time and we were both thrilled to have another little boy. I spent 9 days in the hospital as Shawn recovered from jaundice. Dennis managed to look after Brant but was not available to pick us up from the hospital. Joan Fish was a willing stand-in and we took the baby home to meet his big brother. Brant loved him right from the start and was very good about sharing me with Shawn. First thing in the morning, I would bring the baby into my bed to breastfeed him. This was fine except that Brant would wake up and want his breakfast at the same time. I finally figured out a way he could make his own breakfast and then come into the bedroom and watch TV while I finished with the baby. When he came into ask for his breakfast, I said, "Brant, there's a little glass of milk in the fridge and a little bowl of cereal on the table, get the milk and pour it on the cereal." Brant was able to pour the milk on the cereal and was very proud of himself. The second morning, I explained it to him again, ". . . there's a little glass of milk in the fridge . . . etc. On the third morning, he came into the bedroom and asked "Mom, is there a little glass of milk in the fridge?" After that, he did not ask, but just automatically had his breakfast before he joined us to watch TV.

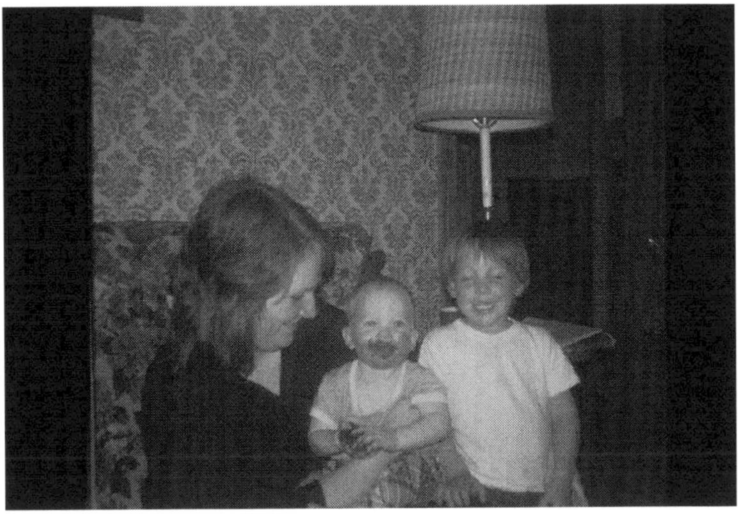

Part Three

Entrepreneurial Training

Shortly after we got settled in Victoria, my cousin Brad from Saskatoon came out to Victoria to set up a satellite financial office for the company he worked for. Growing up we had spent a lot of time together and really got along well. Brad was raised in a very entrepreneurial family and I had no idea that his influence would have such a profound effect on our family and me.

I had already had many cars, and with my engineering training was able to fix most mechanical problems, but Brad wanted to make money buying and selling cars. He knew a lot about the car market and which cars to buy and not buy. We bought the first car in our new automotive joint venture, which was a 1963 Chevy 2. It only needed a few slight repairs and in less than two weeks it landed us a profit of nearly a third of my monthly salary!

Soon there wasn't a day that went by that we didn't have a car for sale, and it wasn't long before we had a car for sale at his place and mine at the same time.

Most of the cars only needed small repairs, but in one case the car was white and had some very noticeable damage to the rear quart panel running from the driver's side back wheel to the rear bumper. So I had to improvise an auto body shop! I went to the hardware store and bought a fiberglass plumbing pipe repair kit and a can of white spay paint. After I filled the crumpled dints and tried to match the original car color with the spray paint, it was obvious the whole car had to get painted. I moved it onto the street so overspray wouldn't get on anything else in the yard, then made a cardboard template the size of one of the wheels, held it in place and began to spray! Hand held masking while spraying is quite an art, but I didn't have time to develop that skill. When it was done, the car looked surprisingly good, until I moved it off the street back to our yard. That's when I saw the imprint of all four wheels outlined in white on the black pavement!

Well, that was nothing that a little flat black spray paint wouldn't cure! And the rest of the flat black spray paint went to good use making the black floor mats look like new too!

Brad was always on the look for good deals and it didn't seem to matter what the commodity was. One day he mentioned he'd seen a trailer in a mobile home park for sale, and thought we could turn it over for real money.

All this was new to me but I was sure on board. We looked at the trailer that was being sold by an old guy who had been told by the park manager that he had to move the trailer away. It was old; 8 feet wide by about 36 feet, skirted all around with a dilapidated built-on porch. A few days of cleaning and painting and we'd be ready to move it to some other park where we would put it for sale.

That's when we found out that no parks would take an 8-foot wide trailer because they were too old and all the new trailers were 12 feet wide and at least 50 feet long. We were in a bit of a panic! Then I realized that it seemed to be an arbitrary decision by the park manager to have it moved, so our only option then was to approach him with a deal.

We told him our sad tale of not being able to find anywhere to move the trailer and that we were desperate. He seemed somewhat sympathetic, so we thought we'd offer him some money. We figured it would cost at least $200.00 to move it anyway, so offered to pay him $300.00 cash, plus a $10.00/month increase in the pad rental if he would allow us to keep the trailer in place. The cash to him was probably 3 times what he was being paid per month to manage the park. While he was considering our offer, I resorted to a trick we often used when buying cars. I pulled out the wad of cash, all small bills and started counting it in front of him. He quickly took the money and agreed. We sold it in a week for more than three times our cost!

We continued to make money on every car deal, and soon Marcia and I had enough money to consider buying our first home. We found a very low priced house located on the far north end of Douglas St. in Victoria. We were now qualified to get a government guaranteed home loan that enabled us to only put up a 5% down payment. We were very excited about the possibilities and started the paperwork, however after a couple of weeks, we were informed that the HOUSE didn't qualify for a CMHC mortgage. It was too old, needed too much work and was in a location that was not suitable for children. We were very disappointed, but in hindsight, the government saved us from completing on a bad decision.

Our First House

We were now committed to finding the right house for us. So I contacted a friend I had sailed with in the navy who got out a few years earlier and was now a realtor. Rick Kallstrom found an older house in Langford beside the Legion on Aprell Place that was on a very large lot. The house had been moved there, so it had been brought up to current building code standards. It was a little more expensive at $36,000.00, but well worth it and thanks to our car sales, we now had enough for that down payment.

Our new mansion was an 850 square-foot 2-bedroom house with a basement that had an 8-foot high ceiling with a ground level exit. It was wide open on each side of the main support beam, and looked just right for a spare bedroom and a workshop. I didn't know anything about building or renovating, but how hard could it be? After all, when I was about 9 years old, I watched my dad do a similar project on our house in Regina.

I bought most of the lumber and all of the doors and frames from a used building materials store which greatly helped keep costs down. I built a spare bedroom, and bathroom along with a nice workshop. Once the basement was finished, I saw the possibility of adding a garage that would greatly add to my workshop capabilities, and the bonus was that I could make the flat roof of the garage into a deck accessible from the kitchen upstairs.

I had to make sure that the finished roof of the garage with a deck surface on it would be level with the kitchen floor inside. Accurate measuring of an interior floor height on an exterior wall would be very difficult, but my engineering training usually kicked in when required. In this case I used a translucent green garden hose filled with water. Marcia sat at the top of the stairs inside holding one end of the hose; I was on the outside on a stepladder holding the other end of the hose. When she held the hose up until the water level was exactly at floor level, she called out and I marked the water level on the wall outside. Again all the structural 2"x 8" floor joists and even the tongue and groove 2" x 6" boards that I used to make the garage doors were recycled.

The Hole

I never liked to be too predictable and always liked to throw some fun into whatever was going on. Like one time in bed when we were both awake, Marcia got up in the middle of the night to go to the bathroom; I turned upside down and had my feet on the pillow. Of course it was dark so when she got back and put her arm over me, she notice something felt different, it was pretty funny when she found she was talking to my feet! Another time the toaster stuck and burned the toast filling the kitchen with smoke and the smell lasted all day. Well the next time it happened, as I ran over to the toaster, I told Marcia to open the door, she expected me to throw the toast out, but I grabbed the toaster and flung it out the door to the back yard with the toast still in it! I never put up with things that don't work properly. When I had the garage finished, I decided to open the wall from the kitchen to what would become our new deck. So I came up the stairs to the kitchen with a sledgehammer and made out that I was chasing a fly. I ran around the kitchen swatting, then turned and ran straight for the wall. I punched a big hole through the drywall and said, "There I got him!"

My favorite unpredictable response from Dennis was when I would ask him to move over a little bit in bed (to give me more room), he would move over a little bit closer! I loved that and to this day, he will unpredictably do the same thing.

I learned another valuable lesson We couldn't afford to pay for tradesmen to do renovations, so it was obvious I had to do them and learn on the job. Even buying materials was a financial stretch, so I made or acquired those as well. I wanted to build a real wood burning fireplace in the house, so I went out to a construction site where they had blasted granite out for the foundation and picked up all the rock scraps I needed to complete the masonry masterpiece! However I found that using drywall scraps to finish the basement ceiling was a bad idea because it left a thousand seams to fill! Well now I had a new problem. How was I going to hide those seams? Hiring a guy to come in with a hopper full of spray on texture was out of the question and do it yourself texture hadn't been invented yet. So I had to find a solution, which started with buying a 40-pound bag of drywall filler, referred to in the trade as "mud". Then I found a construction company that was getting rid of some of their unused old paint, and I got a hell of a deal on it. I mixed the mud with bit of water, added the latex paint to a slurry about the consistency of heavy cream, then for texture, I added rolled oats, tapioca, rice and cracked wheat, all of which were in our kitchen cupboards. I was able to trowel this concoction on to the ceiling covering all the imperfections. When it dried, it was amazing. Hard, solid and sealed! after building the deck. When it was ready for paint, I thought I'd take a shortcut and only do two coats of paint rather than starting with one primer coat. It only took about a year to find what a mistake that was. Because I bypassed the primer coat, the paint didn't adhere to the wood and began to flake off in small sections and resulted in my having to scrape the entire surface in order to undo the mess. It ended up costing me more than double in both time and effort as well as actual hard costs. I never again used cheap paint, because it isn't cheaper, and I never again cut the time by avoiding the proper procedure.

The Trouble With Fire

Now that the garage was a well outfitted workshop with oxyacetylene torch and arc welding equipment I made a burn barrel by arcing holes in a 45 gallon drum to burn all the construction scraps from renovating. I put the barrel in the middle of the yard and filled it with woodcuttings mixed with old newspapers. I didn't want to take the time to peel off sheets of newsprint and I knew they wouldn't burn properly unless I did. But I had another idea, a shortcut! I'd pour gas on the newspaper bundles. I knew gas was very volatile in a closed space, but the barrel had holes. I knew gas was heavier that air and if I used it in the barrel, the vapors could seep out through the holes and surround me in flames. So I was careful to pour the gas quickly and immediately lit the match.

Well, I guess the gas didn't appreciate the holes, and still felt like it was in a contained environment, so it went off like a huge cannon complete with a sound that could be heard several miles away! All of the surrounding neighbors came out to see if a plane had crashed, just in time to see complete sheets of flaming newspaper floating 60 feet in the air in all directions. It was pretty scary, because as the flaming sheets burned they began to descend, but fortunately each sheet burned into a big black flake of flying soot before landing in every neighbor's property. Another shortcut lesson learned.

Finally Doing Well in School

I had finished my last engineering school training program at the top of the class and was therefore eligible for one of six machinist specialist training positions offered only to the top three finishers on each coast. We had to build numerous projects such as: a crankshaft machined from a single block of steel with a 2-piece brass bearing assembly that had to fit perfectly, a steel swivel vice, and several other items that involved critical measurements and extraordinary milling and machining techniques. I found that I excelled at these projects, to the extent that I finished each project days and in some cases weeks ahead of the others in the class, while getting top marks as well. So the instructors allowed me to do any projects I wanted while the others completed their curriculum tasks. I built a wood lathe, a custom brass fireplace tool kit for the fireplace I had recently built at our house, a multispeed drill press and several other handy items that I dreamed up. I finished at the top of that class as well!

OUTSTANDING STUDENT IS MASTER SEAMAN D. Pinvidic is shown receiving acknowledgement for having been named the most outstanding student on his MAR ENG Trade Qualifying Course. Dennis is a native of Regina, Saskatchewan and has been in the Canadian Forces for ten years. He is married, has two children and when not at sea on HMCS MACKENZIE resides here in Victoria.

OUTSTANDING STUDENT AWARD is presented to Master Corporal Dennis Pinvidic of HMCS Mackenzie on completion of recent Machinist Specialist course. Making the presentation is Lieut. Cdr. R. Hahn.

Marching

I liked being an engineer but didn't have much time for the military aspects. One of the things I didn't like was every time there was a military ceremonial function or a street parade for Victoria Day or Buccaneer Days or whatever, they would round up most of the guys from the engineering school to practice marching in formation. Not only did this cut into my time for making personal items but it also cramped my entrepreneurial time as well. It meant that I'd have to get my dress uniform in perfect shape, muster wherever the parade started, march for a mile or two and basically give up an entire day. There was no way to option out; if they called you for parade duty you were done, but I found a way to deal with this major inconvenience. On the parade square where the 100 plus unfortunate selectees would meet to begin sharpening their marching in unison techniques, the drill sergeant would form us into lines of about 8 to10 guys and about twelve columns deep. He would shout, "By the left, quick, march!" This meant everyone leads off with their left foot. This also causes your right arm to swing forward. Of course there were always one or two guys that would get their left and right foot mixed up and catch hell in front of everyone for that. Once we were all marching as a synchronous block it looked like a machine, but I found a way to make it look wrong! After a few steps I would smoothly change my arm swing to have my right arm going forward with my right leg and the left arm matching my left foot. It was subtle but it was noticeable. The drill sergeant noticed, but he couldn't figure out how I would start off correctly and then shortly thereafter end up completely out of synch. He figured it must be some mental problem I had that would cause this incoordination, so he didn't give me a hard time; he just pulled me out of the group and sympathetically told me to go home!

Parade problem solved!

Arm Wrestling

I got drafted to mine sweepers for two years. These were a group of six vintage 130-foot vessels that were all wood, with no magnetic components, so all metal was either aluminum or non-magnetic stainless steel and when under way the hull put up a huge bow wave. Their intended wartime purpose was to defend against mines near the surface of the water that would blow up steel destroyers, but a minesweeper pushing a big bow wave would wash the mines to the side and at the same time the mines would not be attracted magnetically. Now obsolete, a minesweeper's sole purpose was to provide training for young officers in navigation and anchoring techniques. Only four of the six sweepers were in service at any time, while the other two would be in refit.

I reunited with Larry Fish, an engineering friend that I had sailed with years earlier on a destroyer and now our job was simply to keep these boats running. We had a lot of fun because they never went far or for long periods of time. Our night navigation trips were usually cut short when the prop would hit a log and we would have to return for a week or so for repairs.

One day we were at sea near Vancouver when a "Mayday" was broadcast on the emergency radio frequency and it came from a fish boat at the mouth of the Fraser River. Because the fisheries only opened certain areas for a short time, the commercial fishermen had to get all they could catch as quickly as possible, and they would fish around the clock until they were completely full. Apparently, this fisherman had taken on too much fish and was very low in the water when a wave flooded the stern of his boat. After receiving the call, we raced full speed toward his location and by the time we got there, two other boats were helping by pumping out his boat, which had a severe list. Unfortunately, when we stopped quickly in front of him from full speed, our bow wave carried on toward his boat. It immediately swamped the vessel causing it to sink on the spot! The owner was just able to jump to one of the other boats before he went down with it! Everyone there was yelling and screaming at us as we turned and left the scene.

We sailed to many small port towns along the west coast where Larry and I would hustle pool at pubs together so we never had to pay for our drinks, and we raked in the money arm wrestling! Larry was a thin, small built guy and I was surprisingly strong, so we would start arm wrestling in the pub and I would make out like it was very difficult to beat him, then he would take out his wallet and pay me a few bucks. Almost like clockwork someone would come over and ask to take on the winner, after all, if I had that much trouble beating a skinny guy like him, I should be easy to beat. I'd make them put
the money on the table and I would make it look easy or difficult to beat them, whichever seemed most appropriate; but either way they usually wanted to try again, and had to pay each time!

The Worthless Chair

When we would come to a larger port city, we always seemed to tie up at the worst end of town, in an industrial district or some rundown area that was very unsavory and usually a very long walk to civilization. One Friday night, four of us had taken a taxi to the downtown area where we ended up in a very large, crowded pub. After several hours in the pub, we thought it was time to go back to the ship, because we couldn't drink too much more, and I noticed a line of people at the door waiting to get in. It occurred to me that the reason for the line was that all the chairs inside were taken, so calling on my supply and demand instinct; I decided to try auctioning off my chair. I stood up, held the chair over my head and asked for a bid. I started with $5.00. No one responded, so I dropped it to $3.00, and still no takers, so at $1.00 after three tries, I said, "OK, we'll pass it by." I kept the chair over my head and began to walk toward the door, and my buddies followed. I was waiting for one of the bartenders to stop me, but they didn't say a word. We passed the crowd that was waiting to enter and outside, the guys asked what the hell I was going to do with that chair? I really had no idea, and still expected one of the bar staff to come out and get it, but after about five minutes, I realized no one was coming, so obviously the chair had no value to them. It was a very nice solid oak chair and now that it was here, outside with me, I couldn't just leave it. I convinced the guys that we couldn't get it and us in a taxi, so we'd have to take a bus back to the ship! We walked to the nearest bus stop, got on the bus, chair and all, and eventually got back to the ship, where I had to lug it up the gangway. The duty personnel didn't even ask any questions as I passed through carrying the chair. I stashed it in the steering gear compartment and took it home when we got back to Victoria. The chair stayed with us for over twenty years and always held a special place in my mind as a rescued "worthless chair."

Rocking Rocks

At the base stores office, I was able to trade the swivel vise I made as a project during the engineering course for a very large roll of heavy mill plastic vapor barrier, which I intended to use as a weed barrier, covered with crushed rocks in my large yard at home.

After laying out the plastic all over the yard, I had a load of crushed rocks delivered. It was nearly 8 feet high by 20 feet around. This would likely take years to spread by hand and wheelbarrow; I needed to find a shortcut, so I rented a

Bobcat with a front loader. I had never even been near one of these machines, but how hard could it be! The controls for moving forward and back as well as turning, by stopping the wheels on one side, were all done with your feet. Raising, lowering and tilting the bucket were done by hand levers. It was a coordinating confusion, but I got the hang of it fairly quickly. I found that when I got a load of rocks in the bucket, it was difficult to see where I was going, so on the next load, I raised the bucket containing about a ton of rocks to the top of the bucket travel, about 7 feet over my head and began to reverse. As soon as I stopped going backward, which in this machine was abrupt, I was surprised to find that the incredible weight of the rocks in the full bucket over my head didn't want to stop! The Bobcat rocked back until the front wheels came off the ground! I thought I was going to be killed and be buried in one action! Luckily it rocked back and forth several times until all the wheels were back in touch with the ground at the same time — and I had learned another lesson without paying dearly for it.

The Pig

Marcia and I developed a habit of not keeping change in my pocket or her purse. Every time we would get change from a purchase, at the end of the day we would put it in a dish on the dresser in the bedroom. Soon we realized we had to get a neater system for storing the random coins, and as it happened my sister Dianne had given us a piggy bank for our wedding. It was made of pottery, with a slot, but no access hole, which meant that if you wanted to get the money out you had to "break the bank." We put all our change in that pig for well over a year. When we broke it open we had almost $200.00 in it. That's when we decided to glue it back together and this time fill it with all our coins; except from now on, no pennies.

It was amazing how quickly the bank got really heavy and soon we couldn't fit any more coins in the slot. So when the big day came, I gave the side a whack with a hammer and coins spread out for nearly two feet all around the chards of pottery. To our surprise we had saved over $700.00, which was more than I made in a month! Our next steps were obvious; buy Marcia a piano and glue that pig back together again! But unfortunately this time there were too many small pieces, so we couldn't glue it back together, but we always remember "Herman the Pig" fondly.

Part Four

Ending a Career

My cousin Brad went back to live in Saskatoon, and I continued buying and selling cars and had plenty of room for them in my big crushed rock surface yard. After learning how to renovate by trial and error, and with all the tools I had, it seemed logical to start a business. I thought there wasn't anything that I couldn't fix, so I started my first business and called it General Household Repairs. My friend Larry Fish, who had left the navy a few years earlier, was already doing renovation projects, so we partnered up and worked together evenings and weekends doing residential plumbing renovations, basement improvements and deck construction.

I had spent nearly half of my twelve years in the navy in engineering school, but now it was time to go back to a ship and that meant being away a lot. So shortly after getting posted to the destroyer HMCS McKenzie I asked to be transferred to the Air Force. Based on my engineering credentials, the Ottawa-based aviation career manager agreed to take me immediately, however the Navy would not approve the transfer. The Navy feared that if I were allowed to go directly to the Air Force, there would be a flood of similar requests. I told them that if I couldn't transfer I would request a release. I'm sure they didn't believe I would do what I said, especially since I only had to stay eight more years to be pensionable. I think they were very surprised to find I wasn't bluffing and a couple of months later in 1979, I left the navy.

Two weeks after I was officially a civilian, I got a registered letter from The Canadian Armed Forces in Ottawa requesting I report to the Base Chief at CFB Naden in Esquimalt for special consideration. Marcia and I got very little sleep that night as we speculated on what this all meant. We were convinced the military had changed their minds and I would now be transferred to the Air Force. We spent most of that night thinking of the possibilities. Maybe I would get drafted to the air base at Comox, just north of Victoria, which was known to be the gem of all Canadian military bases. How exciting!

When I presented the letter to the Base Chief, he called me into his office and closed the door. His orders from headquarters were to offer me an immediate rank promotion if I would return to the forces and accept an unrestricted posting! Wow! This included an immediate promotion as well! We hadn't even considered that. I asked what an "unrestricted posting" meant. He informed me that as a member of the Armed Forces I could be posted anywhere. I asked if that included a Navy ship? He confirmed that unrestricted meant I could be posted to a ship, and given my training, that was most likely in my future!

I thanked him for the consideration and left to continue my life as a civilian.

CANADIAN FORCES—FORCES CANADIENNES
CERTIFICATE OF SERVICE—CERTIFICAT DE SERVICE
SIN NAS
RANK GRADE
Master Seaman
SURNAME NOM
PINVIDIC
GIVEN NAMES PRENOMS
Dennis Alexis Allan
SERVED FROM A SERVI DU 11 Jul 67 TO AU 29 Mar 79
AND WAS HONOURABLY RELEASED
ET A ÉTÉ LIBÉRÉ HONORABLEMENT

Now that Dennis was home all the time, I looked for something to do for myself. I found Sweet Adelines and started singing with them. It was so much fun and I made friends that I still have today. I had no idea how this decision would change my life.

The house on Aprell was a sweet little two bedroom, and Dennis did renovations to add another bedroom in the basement, along with a shop area. He also added a deck with a garage below. He was pretty good at renovations, so he decided he would get out of the navy in 1979 and start a little business doing household repairs. He could work really hard and did quite well, at one point partnering with our friend Larry Fish. Larry and his wife Joan are our oldest friends and the friendship even survived the dissolution of the partnership.

Partnership

Larry and I were now full time in the renovation business, but weren't making much money. His wife Joan was a teacher with a good salary and they had no kids; Marcia was at home with Brant and Shawn and we had a big mortgage. Larry and I liked working together, but something had to change in order to make more money. I wanted to hire people so we could take on more jobs but Larry was not comfortable with the idea of dealing with employees so I reluctantly suggested we split up because I needed to make more money. We went our separate ways amicably and remained very good friends until his death some 34 years later.

Another good idea I got from Brad was to advertise for things, like: "Wanted, good used car" or "Will pay cash for a Chevy Nova." Ads like that almost always resulted in someone calling because they were inspired to sell when they read the ad. The beauty of this approach was that when I arrived at his or her location, there was no one else competing to buy, so I always got a great deal!

We had built-up some equity in our house over about five years, so I thought it was the right time to look for a property that I could fix up. The ad I put in the paper read: "Young couple looking for a home."

A guy with plenty of financial and family troubles called. His wife had broken both her ankles while trying to escape from him through the bedroom window. And one day while he was out, his wife's new boyfriend came to the house and cut through the kitchen counter with a chainsaw, and removed the built-in dishwasher!

He had a high ratio mortgage, had already missed one payment, couldn't afford any more payments and feared an impending foreclosure. He had tried to list the property with a realtor but the place needed a list of repairs completed before the realtor would even list it.

I listened to his situation and looked at the repair list as well as a couple of items he thought he had fixed. His work was really terrible so I told him not to "fix" anything else. I offered to pay him $1000.00 for everything in the house including the furniture and tools, and take over his mortgage. He thought I'd been sent from heaven to relieve him of all these burdens. The next day I went to the bank that carried his mortgage and asked if I could assume his mortgage. They were happy to replace him with me as a much better covenant.

We closed the deal in just a few days; he moved out leaving a real mess behind. We put our house on Aprell Place up for sale and it sold quickly. Marcia, the boys and I moved in and began renovating what would become our new home on the corner of Hansen and Phelps Avenue.

From the sale of our first house, we now had cash on hand and were living in a newer bigger house with potential that we intended to develop. The first thing we did was build a two-bedroom suite in our ground-level entrance basement and began our first foray as landlords. We made some amazing changes to this place that we knew would come back in spades when it came time to sell.

That got me thinking maybe it was time to look for a new project, so I began advertising for a home. I got a call from a retired guy who had just gone through a divorce and no longer needed a big house. He owned a house on Hampton Road outright and wanted to downsize, but didn't really want a wad of cash that he would have to invest. So I asked if he would like to carry a mortgage; after all I was a youngster with a wife and two kids. He took $10,000.00 down and carried the balance by way of a mortgage.

The deal on our soon to be new home on Hampton allowed us to sell the house on Hansen one year after we moved in. It sold quickly, netting a handsome, tax free profit, however shortly after we moved out, the tenants in the basement suite had a grease fire in the kitchen and the entire house burned to the ground!

We lived at Aprell Place for 5 years and then we began our "moving years." The first house we bought was on Hansen Avenue. It had been badly neglected and we worked hard to renovate it. That house seemed to have a bad aura — shortly after we moved there, a neighbor came by and said that every couple who had lived in it had eventually separated. The place really was a mess and there was evidence of violence and struggle and general unhappiness. As well, the basement had little bits of animals and birds left over from the owner's taxidermy hobby.

Shortly after we moved there, Brant and Shawn wandered off to explore the neighborhood, curious about the wild area near us consisting of forest and rocky outcrops. Suddenly we could hear their screams, and because of the rock face, their screams could be heard all around the neighborhood. We could not tell where the screaming was coming from so Dennis jumped in the car to find them. They came out of the bushes covered with blood and screaming their heads off. Dennis thought a cougar had attacked them, but soon discovered they had been climbing up the rock. They had both fallen — Shawn on his back and Brant on his face. Dennis left the car where it was rather than put the bloody little kids in it and carried them home. A few minutes later, I cleaned them up enough to know that Shawn needed stitches and Brant was in shock — he had a bit of a concussion and while Shawn was stitched up and released, Brant was kept in the hospital for observation. At some point they discovered he also had a greenstick fracture of his arm.

After a year of hard work, we sold the house on Hansen. That house seemed to have a bit of a curse on it. The woman who bought it from us lost her son to suicide while we were in the middle of the real estate deal with her. We had learned a bit more about being landlords because we had a suite in the basement and rented it out to young people. They were noisy, smoked, sneaked animals in and generally disrespected us — of course we were only a few years older than they were. Brant was scared they would burn the house down because they were smokers. It was a bit of a premonition, because shortly after we sold the house the renters caused a grease fire that burned the house to the ground.

Our move took us to 25 Hampton Road, a big old house in town. Once again we set out to renovate and improve the house. Dennis had an incredible amount of energy, working full time and then late into the night to get things done. It's probably why I was so willing to do what we did — Dennis never let things drag on, but set out to do it as quickly as we could. That house was our home for 12 years and our boys still think of it as their childhood home. They often drive by or drop in to check it out.

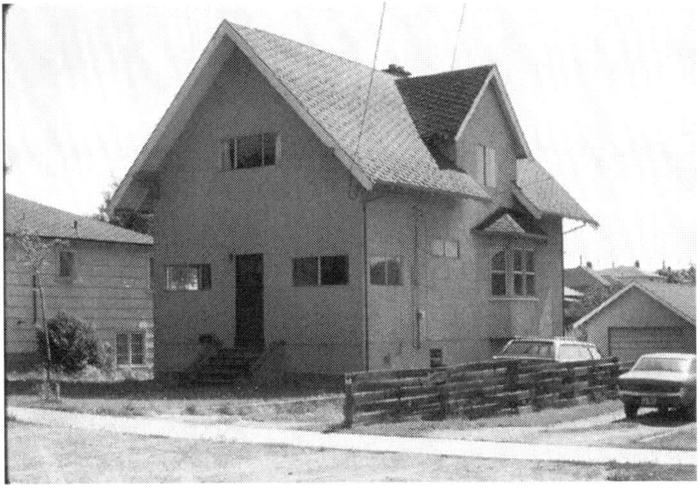

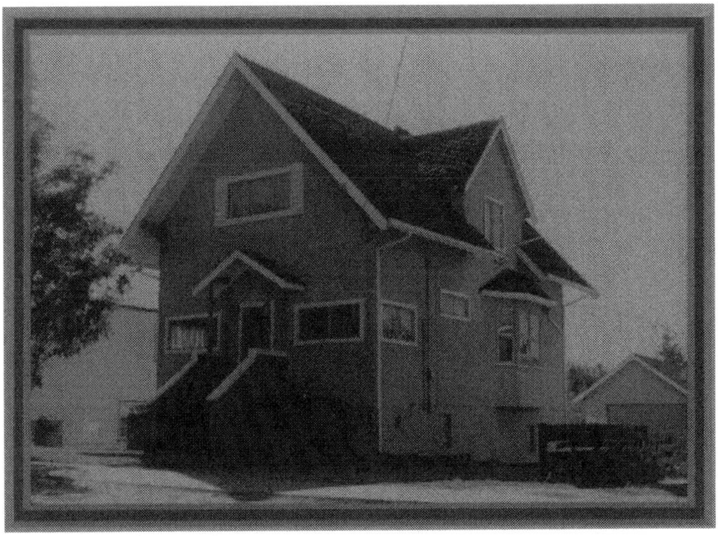

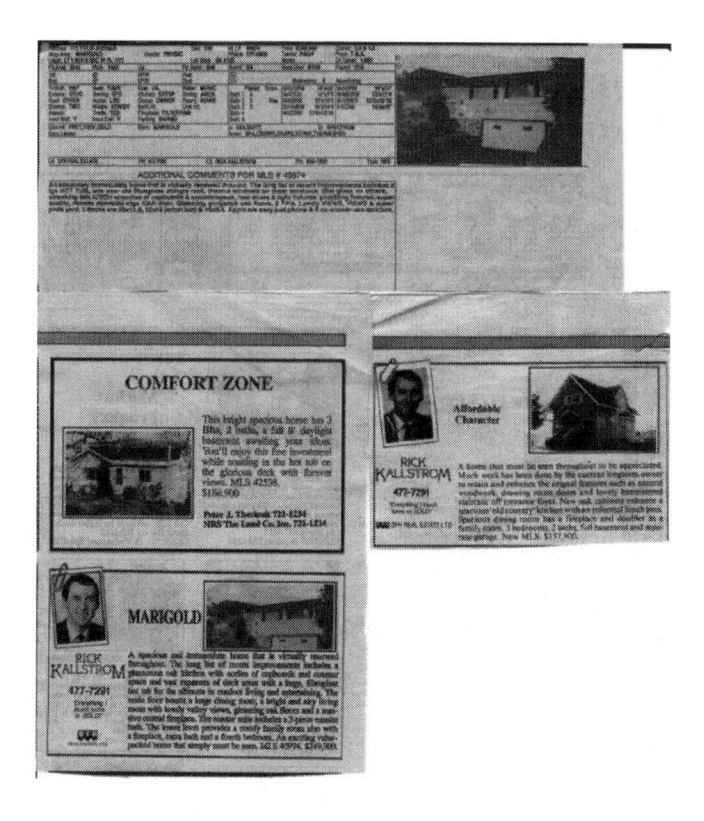

The Landlord Business

In a response to one of my ads, I got a call from an elderly gentleman that had an old duplex at the corner of Viewfield and Old Esquimalt Road. He was fed up dealing with his wife's old spinster friend who for many years had occupied one half. Now that the other side was vacant, he wanted to sell the building, with her in it. He just wanted out, so I was able to negotiate a fabulous cash deal to buy the building, which was constructed as a legal duplex, though the old biddy did come with it.

As soon as I had possession, I got a new tenant in the vacant side at a monthly rent that was nearly twice what the old woman was paying. I went over and introduced myself to her, and explained that I was the new owner and I was going to have to raise her rent. She said, "Oh no you won't sonny." She seemed to know more about the landlord business that I did, and she did! This was when the socialist government of the day had just brought in the policy of Rent Controls. The idea was that the government would restrict landlords from raising rents and that would in theory help the poor people who were predominantly renters. I found myself up against a government bureaucracy as well as the feisty old ex-realtor that knew the rules. I now had a much better understanding of why the previous owner was so anxious to fire-sale the duplex! In order to raise the rent, I had to apply to the Rent Control Board and at my expense, attend a hearing in Vancouver. These bureaucrats were more than happy to deny my application! After all, I was heading toward being a filthy rich landlord.

The old woman that came with the duplex was a constant problem and she certainly helped us make the decision, like the previous owner, to sell the duplex — with her in it — however we still nearly doubled our money.

Welding

It had been difficult making money doing small repair jobs under my General Household Repairs business. In fact one of the final straws was a customer that needed a very special screw built for a rare gun that had lost the adjusting screw for the mechanical sight piece. I had to measure the tiny internal threads and build a screw to fit with a knurled head. I was a trained machinist and had a metal lathe, but it took nearly three hours to make that special screw, and it was small enough to fit on a nickel! I charged the guy $11.00 and he complained that it was a lot for a small screw!

Larry and I were working on various contracting jobs doing carpentry and renovations, but we weren't making much money. I suggested that rather than both of us working at one job, we hire a helper for him and I contract myself out as a welder. We enjoyed working together but something had to change to improve our revenue.

I put the word out, and got a call from Andy, an old Hungarian entrepreneur who was looking for a welder to help build a recycling project in Langford, I was happy to contemplate a better pay check, and started working for him as a welder.

He had a contract to collect all of the scrap copper wire discarded in changing power transmission and telephone cable lines. His plan was to build a huge metal housing on a grid so the plastic coating on the bundled scrap wire could be melted off. The result would be bare copper wire and reclaimable plastic that dripped through the grid floor. The problem was that when plastic burns, it gives off a lot of toxic, black smoke. So he designed a system where the smoke would be sucked up through a three-foot diameter pipe in the roof of the metal housing and bubble through three successive fifteen-foot high water tanks. The water would trap the smoke particulate, resulting in clean air that could be discharged, then the contaminated water would be sent through large swimming pool sand filters. This was a big project that required three full time welders to build. A welding company provided all the equipment and two bodies, and I became the third welder working as an independent contractor for the owner. Along with the normal day-to-day welding, my naval engineer training came in very helpful. A major problem occurred in the three-inch copper water filtration piping only a few weeks after completion. All the lead solder joints in the copper piping began to leak! I remembered how the ships needed 'sacrificial metal' to deal with the electrolysis that occurs when a circulation through dissimilar metals creates a 'battery effect'. I suggested welding large zinc anodes in each water tank so the deterioration would work on the anodes in stead on the lead joints. My solution worked, and from then on I was the go-to guy when any problem arose.

One day I climbed 20 feet up a steel latticework column to arc weld some struts. I had a safety belt sling to hold me while I used one hand to hold the arc rod and the other to hold the strut. I flicked the mask down, began welding, and then suddenly I felt my chest get incredibly hot. I flipped the mask up to find that a molten metal welding spark had landed in the chest pocket of my poly/cotton shirt and caught it on fire. All I could do was stamp it out by whacking my chest with my welding glove, thus matting the burning shirt into my burned skin! I had to take a few days off and that's when Andy, who had recently purchased a 100 acre property, and knowing I was interested in real estate, asked if I would like to work in the office as his property manager. That was the day I hung up the tools for good!

Go Sell It on the Mountain

In order to develop the 100-acre property at the corner of Jacklin Road and the Old Island Hwy. into a residential housing project, I had to get it out of the Agricultural Land Reserve and get the zoning changed. While doing that, I met with several housing developers with the idea of selling off a few 10 to 15 acres parcels. One of the developers was Knute Johnson, of KC Johnson Construction, who had a very good reputation for quality residential projects, but he was not interested in my venture because he had just taken on the development of Mt. Washington Ski Resort. However one day he contacted me and asked if I would come to his office. I thought, well finally now he is interested in my project, but to my surprise he wanted me to come and work for him! As it turned out, I had just completed the zoning hurdles on my project and was looking at taking a well-deserved holiday, but he wanted me immediately, so I respectfully declined.

He had built the day lodge at Mt. Washington in the previous ski season and had a list of people that had expressed an interest in purchasing a ski condo. The plan was to pre-sell and build sixty-six ski condos in the summer before the snow falls, and in order to avoid real estate commissions he needed someone to work directly for him who knew a bit about construction and could sell.

When I told him about my holiday plans, he said, "What if I make you an offer you can't refuse?" The next day, on my 30th. birthday, in 1980, I started working for him at $5K/month!

He had a spare office for me with a phone and a secretary chair, not even a desk. I took his list of skiers, put the phone on my lap, and started making calls.

I had never skied or even been to the project that I was now pre-selling at $70,000.00 per unit, but things started to go very well, especially considering there was no way anyone could get a mortgage on condos that were not yet built and were going to be built on leased land!

All purchasers had to put up a non-refundable $2,000.00 down payment to secure their purchase and pay progress payments through the construction phase until the anticipated completion in October.

When I finally got to see the property that I was selling at Mt. Washington, I realized why all these well-to-do people were putting cash down on the condos we were going to build.

That's when I thought, if these guys are doing it, maybe we should as well! And fortunately, by now we had enough cash ourselves to do it, so we did.

I think Knute was pretty surprised when I returned from the mountain and said we were going to buy one! By October of 1980 all 66 of the flat-roof units that I had sold were completed, and fully paid for; an accomplishment that would be nearly impossible to duplicate in most people's lifetime.

I had several people ask if I would coordinate some kind of furniture package for the condos, so I contacted the only reputable company that I knew that could handle that kind of undertaking. It was Eaton's Contract Sales. The senior sales guy was very happy to entertain an order of that size, however he stipulated it had to be at least 20 full three-bedroom furniture and accessory packages in order to get the best price. Marcia and I had just purchased the house on Hampton Rd, so the 21st package went there. We could finally have some "new" furniture at home. The packages included everything you would need to just move in, right down to sheets, towels, cutlery, pots, lamps and toilet paper.

Unfortunately it was a real shock when all the fully loaded Eaton's trucks arrived at the mountain and found that the ski village didn't have roads between the buildings, so it involved a lot more carrying. What made it worse was that it was November and some snow had already fallen thus it was a mud pit!

I went up to the mountain just after everything had been delivered to make sure I could sign off on the completion and authorize final payment to Eaton's. I found that nearly every piece of furniture came packed in cardboard, including the beds, end tables etc. and all the cardboard containers were piled up outside each building.

I had a helper with me, but rather than do several small controllable fires, I thought we'd take a shortcut and just make one bigger one. So we gathered and flattened all the cardboard from around the other seven buildings, piled it into one big heap in a clearing in the trees near the largest building, Bldg. #85. The flattened cardboard scrap heap was about eight feet tall and nearly 15 feet around. I made sure we had at least 20 feet of clearance from any combustibles in all directions before I lit it on fire. I had no idea that due to the nature of the construction of cardboard with its endless corrugated tunnels each one acted as an air supply tube for what turned out to be a blast furnace. Once the mountain of cardboard got fully engulfed, it sounded like a roaring turbine, and I realized we had no control over the flames that were now rising about 40 feet in the air! We had no way to do anything; we didn't even have a water hose. When I heard the tree tops start snapping from the heat I thought, wow, we just finished this project and I'm going to be responsible for burning it to the ground before anyone even moved in! Fortunately the flames began to decline just before the trees caught fire and I realized I'd dodged another bullet!

I had to form the new strata councils for each of the condo buildings and get those running as part of our turnover to the owners, and at the same time the Mount Washington Ski Resort Ltd. was organizing their own strata, so I became part of the original Strata Plan 799 strata council.

We took up skiing as a family that first year and spent nearly every second weekend of the ski season for the next twelve years having great times. Both Brant and Shawn would become expert skiers and have many powerful bonding opportunities that would remain a core of their uniquely close relationship.

One weekend on Sunday afternoon, we got a dump of about 16 inches of new snow. It covered everything so thoroughly that cars parked in the lot at the top of the mountain looked like small bumps similar to moguls and it was just impossible to dig out, so I told the boys we would stay to ski on Monday and they wouldn't be going to school. I was surprised that they liked school, and this news didn't affect them the way it would have for me, had I ever been in their position!

My parents visited Victoria several times in winter over the years and finally, in 1981, when my youngest brother Allan finished high school, they decided to move to Victoria permanently. Allan, who was only four years old when I left for the navy, was now 18. He and I really got along well and though we were already brothers we now became friends. He was the one in our family who was just like my dad, and that is a rather big compliment. He has the same temperament, and ironically, like my dad, loves Barber Shop singing as well!

Allan had worked part time at the TV station in Regina and was hoping to get a job in that field on the west coast, so he submitted an application to CHEK TV in Victoria, but had not heard from them.

The summer following our first ski season, I brought a small construction crew including Allan up to the mountain to deal with defects, repairs, modifications and retrofits that emerged or had been requested by the new owners. At that time the only way to communicate in isolated environments was to carry a rather expensive radiophone and link through the land-based telephone operator. When Allan told me about his wish to work at CHECK TV, I thought maybe we could impress the boss there by initiating a radiotelephone call, which I knew very few people had ever experienced.

I called the BC TEL radiophone operator, who in turn called the telephone operator, who then called CHEK TV and announced "I have a radiotelephone call from Mt. Washington for the general manager."

Someone at CHEK ran around, found the GM and he took the call. I explained where we were calling from and that Allan was there working for me, but wanted to work at CHEK and his resume was already there. I asked him if he would like to speak to Allan and handed over the radio. Needless to say, the GM was quite impressed, and while he was on the call, he located Allan's application. He asked a few questions and set up an appointment to meet upon Allan's return. Allan got the job and has subsequently worked in the visual media field for his entire career.

The First Marcia's Den

While I was working up on the mountain in the summer of '81, Marcia and the kids came up a few times to stay in our new ski condo, which we cleverly called Marcia's Den. We had a beautiful new Oldsmobile Cutlass and because the roads were gravel, I brought the van down to meet them at the parking lot at the base of the mountain where we would leave the car for the weekend. Unfortunately one time we came down on a Sunday evening to find that some vandals had broken every window on the car, and smashed the headlights and taillights as well as kicked dents in the doors. It was a very traumatic experience, but I'm still glad I didn't catch the guys that did it, because I'd probably still be in jail today.

After the car was fixed we never left it down in the isolated parking lot again but that didn't interfere with our plans to have fun as a family on the mountain, or in the woods. Our first summer adventure into the surrounding forests was hiking to one of the lakes within five miles of the ski hill, however we found it was not quite as nice as we anticipated. The air was thin and we all got quickly sunburned, the bugs were plentiful and clearly loved having a family of humans to eat. It seemed that no matter what species of flying insect, they all had a very effective communication system amongst themselves, because they apparently flew over from many miles away to try the new tasty human meals being served. When we finally got to our destination lake there was no beach — it was swampy mud with fallen rotten trees forming an obstacle course to the water, and when we finished traversing the last obstructions to our well deserved dip in the pristine clear lake water we were shocked, and I mean literally shocked to find the water temperature at only 5 degrees above freezing!

We immediately turned around and headed back to the condo. When we arrived, we were exhausted, sun burnt, raw with bug bites, and both kids were not feeling well. Brant had the signs of sunstroke so we packed up and headed straight back to Victoria. On the way while going through the back roads from the mountain toward Courtenay, a car got behind me and was tailgating for several miles when Shawn called out from the back seat, he was going to be sick. I told him to make sure he didn't throw up in the car. He no sooner rolled down the rear passenger window when it came roaring out! I saw through the rear view mirror a cloud form just behind our car and land directly in the middle of the tailgater's windshield. It happened very fast, and I didn't even slow down as the car behind faded back into the distance.

Tick Removal

When we got home, Brant complained about something stuck on his head. I began to look for the source of his discomfort by searching through his hair like a grooming monkey. Then there is was. It was the first time I'd ever seen a tick. It had burrowed its head in under his scalp and its rear was protruding. I had heard that if you heat a needle and touch the rear end of the tick the irritation would cause them to dislodge. Again, resorting to my theory of "If a little is good, more is better," I thought it would be difficult to maintain any kind of significant heat on the end of a small needle, so I came up with a shortcut, that would be way better! I didn't understand that the hot needle was intended to be an irritant not an evisceration tool, so I went to my toolbox and brought out the soldering iron! Marcia was very uncomfortable to say the least. I said, "I know it could be a little dangerous, but if you hold Brant's head very still, I can do it."

Brant was too young to understand the risk he was being subjected to, and I think both he and Marcia had somewhat unfounded confidence in my abilities. As Marcia got Brant prone on the couch and I rigged extension cords as we prepared for the operation. I got the tip of the soldering iron smoking hot while Marcia held Brant's head in a death grip. She separated out his hair and exposed the tick's ass. As soon as I touched the bug, it fried on the spot and because it was now dead, made no effort to back out! Well the first part of this extraction didn't go as planned, so I got the needle nose pliers and grabbed what was left sticking out of Brant's scalp and gave it a gentle tug, which quickly separated the tick into two equal parts one half in the jaws of my pliers and one buried in Brant's head. At that point, it was clear I had expended all of my medical surgery options, so we got in the car, drove to the emergency clinic and had the remains cut out by a doctor.

New Ups and Downs

I had sold Mt Washington condos to a very wide array of individuals and maintained ongoing communications with most of the owners, especially during the first year. Initially I had to turn some potential purchasers away because all the units had been sold. But in 1981, the real estate market had risen dramatically as well as interest rates. Several new owners wanted to flip their ski condo and approached me to re-sell their unit. The original price only three months earlier of $70,000.00 had now risen to well over $100K. I handled the sale of several successful flips, and even considered flipping ours as well. In one case I decided to conduct the deal in another unit because I didn't want the new purchaser to see how much nicer my condo was. That's when I decided to keep ours and maybe even try skiing, then consider selling since it would likely double in value by next year!

When interest rates went to 21%, those owner/investors that had borrowed the money to purchase found it impossible to carry the burden. Soon, as desperation set in, fire sales began to occur. The real estate market was crashing everywhere but mostly in Victoria and Vancouver. Now you could buy one of our ski condos, for under $60,000.00! Fortunately we had a stable, fixed mortgage on our personal residence and owned the ski condo outright. The real estate market was really crashing all over, and the areas that had benefited the most from fast rising prices were now getting hit hardest with the biggest declines.

It was very clear that working in the real estate market was going to be pretty dry for the foreseeable future, but just then, the general manager of Montgomery Elevator Co., who had purchased one of our condos, asked me if I would consider working for him.

It was an easy decision and in 1982 I started a new career in service / sales with Montgomery Elevator, a job that seemed perfectly suited for my engineering and sales background.

Though spending time at the mountain in the summer didn't turn out, I still thought we needed something to do in the summer as a family, so I bought a Hobie Cat! That is a watercraft consisting of a tall sail, two pontoons with trampoline stretched between them. I had never sailed before but how hard could it be?

I practiced setting it up on its trailer beside the house and looked forward to getting to the beach to test this beast out.

I brought Allan with me to Elk Lake and set it up at the boat ramp just down from the public beach. So there it was sitting there with the wind trying to get it going without us. It was then that I realized I had no idea what to do next and I sure wasn't going to launch this in the water to learn the next steps.

I left Allan to guard it while I took the car back to the main beach. I started walking along the shore calling out to the sunbathers, "Does anyone know how to sail?"

One young guy said he did and I asked if he would come with me to do a little tutoring. He agreed to come with me, so we jumped in the car and went back to the waiting sailing machine. The three of us got on the "Cat" and swished off. He showed us a few maneuvers as we sailed toward the public beach. Then all of a sudden, he said, "OK you're on your own now," jumped off and swam to shore! Allan and I learned to sail that day by immersion, and we both became boaters!

The Superintendent at Montgomery, Don Fischer, was a real boater and invited Marcia and I to join him, his wife Rita and all our kids for a weekend at an island called Sidney Spit, just north of Victoria. I was happy to accept, but I was going to bring my own boat. We brought a tent, sleeping bags, cook stove and everything a family of four would need for a month. We had so much gear, it filled a rubber raft that we towed behind the Hobie Cat, but fortunately there was a good breeze and we made the 4-mile journey in quick time.

It was a fun weekend, and then on Sunday just after noon, the wind came up so I thought we would get a head start. We packed up everything and set out on our return trip. We quickly got about half way when the wind died to zero and the current kicked in; in the wrong direction, of course!

The four of us languished on the 5x6 foot trampoline for over two hours making no progress, when just about the time the real boaters came out to rescue us, the wind picked up and we were finally able to make our way home. When we got back, I vowed this would never happen again, so I sold the Hobie Cat and started looking for a real boat.

The "Flip"

By now I was looking at moving from car sales to focusing on real estate, and was always looking for a deal. One day I saw an ad for a low priced condo on Inverness Road, a poorly built project with lots of low-income renters. I could see that it was offered below market value, so I put in an offer. I had no emotional interest in this condo, so it didn't matter if I got it or not. I found that the best deals are always made when you really don't care! I was surprised when they accepted the low price I offered. My plan was to do a quick flip, so once all the paperwork was complete, I immediately told the realtor to put it back on the market for $10,000.00 more. The realtor was embarrassed to find that he had obviously undersold it to me, when it sold again in a month at full price.

Nearly a year later, I was informed that one monthly strata fee had been missed during the month I owned the unit and the strata council had been levying a fine of $25.00/month. The same property management company had managed the property the entire time, and therefore they were responsible for paying all appropriate fees. Also the law requires that the strata council sign a form ensuring no outstanding fees are due before a unit can change hands. So I was very confident when I told the strata council I was not responsible for the missed payment. However they decided to file a Small Claims action against me, and they also named the property management company and the law firm that handled the title conveyance. I knew I was not in the wrong so I decided to fight the action, and when I went to court, the other defendants joined me. I was shocked when the judge summarily dismissed them and found me, and only me fully responsible for the missed payment, as well as all subsequent fines and collection costs. I knew there was something wrong here, so I filed an appeal to the higher Provincial Court of Appeals. I subsequently won my appeal and the lower court was overruled because the strata council had never informed me about the missed payment or given me a chance to mitigate the damage, so all the costs and fines reversed. My day in court was very exciting and gratifying, however it turned out to be much less eventful than what happened with my dad that day.

Dad

My dad was thoughtful and kind; one of those rare genuinely good people. That truth was proven many times over the years. He was just a retail clerk who had risen to the lofty position of managing "Menswear" at the Sherwood Co-op, a department store in Regina Saskatchewan. He had been offered the opportunity to advance but was happy doing what he knew, he didn't embrace stress and didn't want the strain of doing things he didn't want to do. He really wanted to avoid being promoted to the highest level of his competence, or lack of it. He was certainly not entrepreneurial, but he had a remarkable attitude about doing good work; a virtue that was a challenge for me. Dad didn't perceive his value from his employment status; he loved the other parts of his life best, which included his devotion to mom. He was fluent in French, yet had no accent at all, and as a young man was an announcer on a French radio station. He was also an amazing singer and had recorded several records, so he was always in demand as a master of ceremonies or to sing at weddings. He directed the church choir and loved being part of the international male barbershop singing groups originally part of the Society for the Preservation and Encouragement of Barbershop Quartet Singing in America (SPEBSQSA), now called the Barbershop Harmony Society,

Dad was always willing to help me on my real estate projects with painting, cleaning etc. So when he heard I was going to go to handle my own defense at the Appeals Court, he and Marcia planned to be in court to watch. On the day of my hearing, I arrived at the courthouse early and found that my case was postponed for two hours so I went out the Blanchard St. exit, which was the best vantage point to wait and watch for Dad and Marcia to arrive.

As soon as I got out to where I could see the street, I saw a crowd forming at the corner. I saw Marcia looking back but dad wasn't with her. I went over to see what was going on and when I got there, from behind a few people I saw my dad lying on the sidewalk, he was not moving, and no one else seemed to be doing anything!

He was clearly unconscious and his skin was un-naturally white. I pushed through the crowd and knelt beside him. I had some training in artificial resuscitation in the navy so I lifted the back of his neck which tilted his head back, and began blowing into his mouth. I was surprised to find that all the air I was providing was just come out his nose. That's when I remembered a few more details, like pinch the nostrils shut and begin chest compressions. It was amazing, there was a crowd of about 20 people all standing in a circle, and I was the only one there doing anything. I was still down there alone with him when I looked up and told a guy to come and help. I put the guy's hands one over the other on dad's chest and started pushing a rhythmic pumping. I told him to keep doing it while I carried on with the breathing routine. Shortly after that I saw the color come back to dad's face and he began to regain consciousness. The ambulance and emergency team arrived just then and took over. He went straight into intensive care at the hospital and a few days later had a heart valve replacement operation that ultimately gave him 5 more years of quality life.

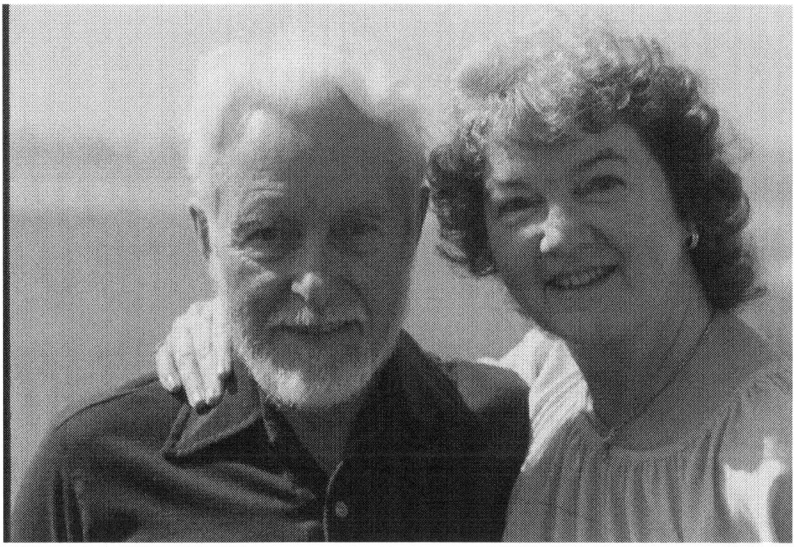

Henri Joseph Pinvidic

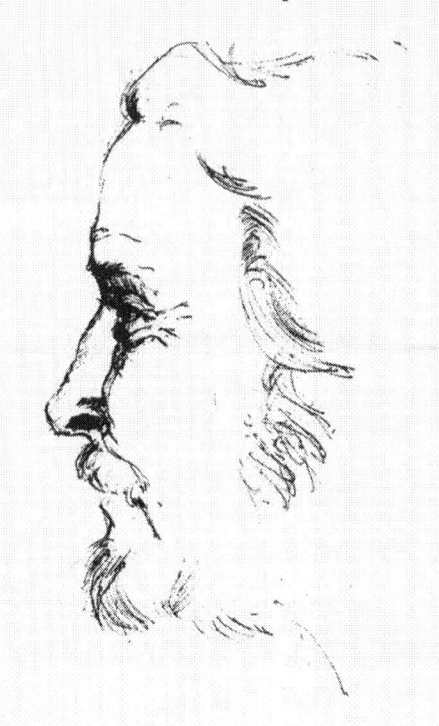

January 5, 1912 – June 8, 1989

Part Five

A New Door Opens

As the Sales/Service Rep for Montgomery Elevator, I made it my mission to become friends with every property manager on Vancouver Island, and get to know who owned and/or operated any building over three floors. It wasn't long before I was the "go to guy" for anything relating to elevators, and our maintenance base began to increase dramatically until eventually we reached nearly 60 percent of the entire market share.

One day a property manager who had a few buildings with overhead doors on their underground parking areas asked if Montgomery would do maintenance on their overhead garage doors. I asked Montgomery's head office and was told they were not interested in a diversion from their core business. I think the fact that the elevator companies were heavily unionized was a significant barrier to branching out to a new field like overhead doors. When I told that to the property manager that Montgomery would not be able to provide maintenance of the doors, she recalled that I had an engineering background and asked if I would do it?

I spoke to our Superintendent and together we decided to start our own overhead door repair and maintenance company, which we called Depend-a-Dor.

Shortly after incorporating the company, I let all the property managers know we were in business and we started doing overhead door maintenance for most of them. That meant we started working most evenings and weekends. "Secure" underground parking became more and more popular not only with new buildings, but existing buildings with underground parking needed overhead doors as well, so we had to learn on the job how to install these commercial grade overhead doors and soon became experts.

We ran the business for a couple of years from home with our wives taking calls and doing the books, but we needed a better space, so we bought a 60-foot shipping container and dropped it in the back yard of our house on Hampton Road.

We modified the container into a very functional warehouse and office, which worked well for a few more years, but we soon needed more space and a real warehouse. I negotiated a very good deal with a rent-to-purchase option on our first warehouse from a developer I knew through the elevator business. The agreement stated that half of the rent in our lease would be credited toward the down payment, if we chose to exercise the option to purchase at an agreed purchase price, within two years. Over the next year and a half our down payment value silently accrued, while the warehouse value nearly doubled. So we exercised the option to purchase and got the warehouse for basically half of the market value. A few years later, as an investment my partner and I bought two more identical strata warehouses in the same complex on Dunsmuir Road.

I enjoyed my job at Montgomery and even though I seemed to be working all the time doing overhead door maintenance evenings and weekends, we loved to get out as a family on the boat whenever we could. It helped that the GM at Montgomery and my partner at Depend-a-Dor, who was also the superintendent at Montgomery, were both boaters and members of Capital City Yacht Club (CCYC).

From Hobie to "Homie"

After enduring the exposure and drifting over the ocean experience on the Hobie Cat, we got our first real 23-foot sailboat which we also called Marcia's Den! It was a very cramped way for 4 people to go camping on the water. But now with a real boat we qualified to join CCYC, and we did in 1985.

The boat had only five feet of total height in the cabin, but we really liked it. We had all the camping gear on board including a naphtha (white gas) cook stove and a portable toilet. At the end of a weekend, as we were returning to our dock at Thunderbird Marina, a guy saw us all on deck and asked if we had actually spent the entire weekend on that little boat? We didn't think it was all that bad but "Yes!" Well, this guy had just purchased a new 33-foot sailboat and intended to sell his 24-foot Bayliner Buccaneer, so he offered us a trial weekend on it for free. This boat had six feet of headroom, a built in stove and salt-water head, so it was a no-brainer; it became our new Marcia's Den for the next eight years.

Hey Hockey Stick:

Not long after getting our new, larger Marcia's Den, I wanted to make the cockpit more hospitable during inclement weather. So I thought I'd build a hard top on the boat with a glass windshield over the hatch and forward part of the open aft deck. I wanted to make it strong enough to so I could stand on it, and that meant it needed a very strong frame. The only way to accomplish that without using large beams was to use laminated wood. That's when I remembered seeing all those discarded hockey sticks at the skating arena. The shaft of a wooden hockey stick is incredibly strong because it is made of laminated wood. When a stick breaks, it is usually at the blade, leaving a useless handle to be discarded. I went to the local arena and asked if I could take all the broken sticks they had stacked in a bin. They were happy to have me rid them of that litter! I made the entire hard top frame structure from hockey sticks with plywood sheathing, and then painted and fiberglass coated it. It wasn't long before the word got out at our yacht club that there was another use for broken hockey sticks, and from that time on, one of my boating buddies always referred to me as "Hockey Stick", even when he called me on the VHF radio!

We spent many weekends and holidays exploring all of the Gulf and San Juan Islands and spent nights in nearly every anchorage. I bought an SUV and had a tandem wheeled custom trailer built to carry the boat, which had a 6-foot dinghy hanging on davits off the rear. This allowed us to take the boat on the west coast of Vancouver Island via the Port Alberni Inlet to the Broken Group of islands between Bamfield and Ucluelet, and also north of Campbell River to Telegraph Cove.

One day while sailing near Malcolm Island in Johnstone Straight, rather than dropping anchor for the night, I thought we'd take a shortcut, so I tied the boat to a huge log boom. That allowed the kids to run around and play on the logs. At about midnight a tugboat crew that was preparing to hook up the log boom awakened us, saying we had to untie because they were going to move the boom. We asked where they were taking it? Their destination happened to be in the general direction we planned to head the next day, so we asked if we could just stay tied up and tag along. They didn't have a problem with that, so we went back to sleep and woke up the next day at Minstrel Island!

After being members of CCYC for a few years we finally got enough seniority to bring our boat into the yacht club moorage. It was a very convenient location and from there we could easily be at some island or anchorage in a couple of hours. One of our favorite spots, about ten nautical miles from CCYC, located just past the tip of Saturna Island near Tumbo Island, was a marine park at Cabbage Island. We could always catch fish and get lots of Dungeness crabs there. The water was shallow and relatively warm for swimming, and it had a nice beach as well as free government mooring buoys. Going there through the extremely narrow passage at Winter Cove was a new and scary learning experience, especially when I got talked into disregarding the tidal flow in the pass! My friend with
the big powerboat convinced me that he could tow us through the pass no matter what. That was when we both

learned what a boat's "hull speed" means. As you try to push a displacement hull boat beyond its hull speed, it simply makes a bigger bow wave and the boat begins to sink lower in the water behind the wave, until if continued, the boat sinks! We could have gone through the pass "with the tide" or at "slack tide," but decided on a shortcut so we wouldn't have to leave early. The shortcut was that we could relax a little longer at anchor and even though we couldn't normally go against the tide flow in the pass, our friend's big powerboat would pull us through. When we finally headed to the pass, the tide flowing against us was approaching 5 knots and we weren't even at the narrowest point where the flow is even faster, so it was clear we weren't going to get through on our own. Our "big boat buddy" was just ahead of us and threw me a line. I kept my engine running, in gear, and at full speed as we headed into the fastest flow of the narrow pass. My maximum speed was about 6 knots and soon we found that no matter how much I revved my engine, and he pushed his throttle until black smoke poured from his exhaust, we did not, and could not go any faster, in fact all that happened was we were stuck in the middle of the pass while getting lower in the water. Fortunately we finally did get through, but that was just as the waterline reached the top of our gunnels!

Brant and Shawn loved our summer boating adventures, which were a nice continuation from our winter skiing adventures that began when they were just 7 and 5 years old. They both became as proficient on the water as they were at skiing.

Many times in the morning while Marcia and I slept in, they would take the dinghy out to fish and check the crab trap and always came back with food. One morning they had been gone for over two hours and when I saw them returning, both boys were standing on the dinghy seats. They had found a small bay with a sand bar that dried at low tide, causing the small bay to turn into a tide pool. The bay was full of crabs and as the tide lowered, the crabs began migrating over the sand bar before getting trapped in the pool. Brant and Shawn stood on the sand bar and just grabbed the big ones as they approached and tossed them into the dinghy. When the boys got back into the dinghy, they had so many crabs they couldn't put their feet on the bottom of the boat!

Brant and Shawn seemed to spend as much time in the little dinghy as on the main boat, however one afternoon we got very concerned because they had been gone for several hours. They were out in a main shipping channel, where waves and currents can easily overpower a 6-foot dinghy with a one and a half horsepower outboard motor. We were at a small anchorage where there isn't enough room for each boat to swing around on their anchor, so all boats tied back to shore. Just about the time I was getting ready to pull up the anchor to go looking for the kids, we heard the welcome sound of that little outboard come putt-putting around the corner into the bay. As they pulled in front of our boat, I asked why they had been gone so long. Brant said, "the fish weren't biting much," then Shawn stood up and said, "We got a really big one, it was nearly 4 feet long, but it got away." Brant said, "Oh, he's lying," then he stood up and lifted a fish nearly 4 feet long, "It didn't get away!" They caught the fish but didn't have a net large enough to pull it up into the boat. They knew they couldn't lift it by the hook or they would lose it. So they waved down a passing boat that helped them net and land it.

O'Boys

One time shortly after we got our new boat, my younger, middle brother, Mark came out to Victoria for a visit so we three brothers set out for a weekend at Bedwell Harbour on Pender Island.

With little else to do but drink, by late Saturday night we were quite saturated. We had a campfire on the beach that was attended by anyone that wandered by and one of the stragglers happened to be a crewmember of a British 140-foot yacht anchored in the bay. At approximately 2:00AM when everyone had gone, we decided to row back to our boat and get some sleep. But as we rowed out we had to go around the big ship, which happened to have a 20-foot long boarding staircase going down from the upper deck to just above the waterline! It looked like an invitation to me, so I suggested we go aboard and visit the new friend we had met earlier at the campfire!

We climbed to the top of the staircase expecting to be greeted by a watchman, like you would find on a navy destroyer, but there was no one there. Mark and Allan were already quite uncomfortable and ready to get back in our boat before getting caught, but I thought, well we're here now, let's have a look around. The brothers stayed cringing by the gangway exit as I walked forward expecting the main access door to be locked. To my surprise it wasn't! I walked in, turned back, stuck my head out and said, "Oh Boys," beckoning them with a finger gesture to advance and follow. As we proceeded to wander the massive ship, I fully expected to run into someone on guard, but it was like the ship was abandoned. We explored the entire ship's interior, even walking through the crew's quarters where everyone was snoring! When we eventually stumbled into the galley, where we were happy to find many meal options, but settled for simply making a couple of sandwiches. By this time it was nearly 4:00AM and as we had completed our tour, we found our way back to the accommodation ladder. It was at that point where we finally ran into a rather shocked crewman! Through mutual agreement we quickly left the ship and rowed back to our boat.

The next day while reminiscing our unbelievable drunken adventure, which now carried the moniker "the O'Boys Tour," we agreed never again to put ourselves in a position of either being shot or imprisoned! We did pledge however to relive an O'Boys Tour every year from then on. Mark, Allan and I have kept that O'Boys Tour pledge, by reuniting somewhere, every year, for well over thirty years.

Sight Unseen

The real estate market was very depressed following the major crash of 1982 and many general contractors had gone out of business — even well established developers were caught with buildings in various stages of construction that could not proceed because new sales dried up and many other purchasers just walked from their deposits. The market was flooded with condos that weren't selling. Montgomery Elevator Co. was owed many thousands of dollars from several developers and contractors who had purchased an elevator for their project, but now couldn't complete. In one case Montgomery took ownership of a condo in lieu of payment for the elevator at Maplewood Place, a condo building in Courtenay up island.

Montgomery carried this condo for a couple of years, which was now worth much less than the original elevator invoice, and the holding costs including property taxes and management fees were a constant irritant. One day I heard the GM discussing with Montgomery's head office a plan to get rid of it, so I offered to purchase it, sight unseen. They were happy to have it go quickly and without real estate fees. I ended up getting it for less than half the original price.

About a year later, the general manager at Montgomery told me he had also purchased a condo on Henry Avenue in

Sidney as an investment, but now that it was worth less than half the original value, wanted out. I offered to buy his unit sight unseen for cash. It was a low offer but it would be quick, out of his hair and would save him the real estate fees. Shortly thereafter we added his condo to our growing real estate portfolio.

Knowledge is Power

I had learned that when making any major purchase, it was very important to find out as much as possible about the vendor; why were they selling, what did they intend to do with the money and anything else that would help tailor an offer. An opportunity arose when an old 50's duplex on the corner of Esquimalt and Lampson came up as part of an estate sale. Settling the estate had dragged on for several months, and the beneficiaries had no interest in keeping the building, which was now in a state of disrepair and one side was vacant. I met with the selling agent and asked a lot of questions in order to get the knowledge I would need to craft the right kind of offer. With the information I had gleaned from the realtor, I submitted a clean and quick offer. I had no emotional investment in this project but the beneficiaries of the estate did, which became obvious when they countered surprisingly close to my offer, which was roughly 40% less than the market value they were asking. It was clear that they simply wanted to dispose of it, so it was easy to come up with the right number on which we agreed.

I renovated both sides, by adding a second bedroom in each basement, upgraded the bathrooms, put new tile floors and countertops in the kitchens, and sanded and refinished the hardwood floors throughout. Doing all the work myself really kept the costs down, however I quickly learned that when using a commercial floor sander, you better keep moving or you'll sand a hole through to the basement in short order! This rental building produced a very nice return for over 20 years until a developer offered to purchase it for nearly four times the original purchase price. That's when we knew it was time to let it go.

The Trades

After a few years of rental turnovers at the condo on Henry Avenue, I began to think about reducing the hassle of having to drive out to Sidney BC to show the unit, so we decided it was time to sell. I put one of my typical ads in the paper saying it was available for sale or trade.

I got a call from an old woman who wanted to downsize and move from her 3-bedroom house on Maxine Lane in Cordova Bay to a condo in Sidney, where she would be closer to her daughter. The situation was too perfect to pass up, so I made a deal to trade the condo for her house plus some cash. The plan was to renovate it and move in.

In the mean time we were still advertising to "buy a home," and only days after the ink dried on the condo trade deal I got a call from a carpenter who wanted to sell his house on Tulip Avenue. I went over to meet him and see the house. I asked as many questions as I could in order find out his needs. He had to sell this house so he would have the money to finish building his new house on the other side of town, which he intended to move into. The house on Tulip was just what we were looking for. It had vaulted ceilings, private back yard, double garage and an unfinished basement. His problem was, he needed about $10,000.00 cash, that he didn't have, and he needed to live at the Tulip location until the new house was completed about 2 months hence. Knowing that I could satisfy his needs, I offered him $10,000.00 in non-refundable cash that he could have immediately, and his family would continue to live in the house until the deal closed in 2 months, however he would have to take a big hit on the purchase price. My offer was just what he needed and though he really didn't like the price, he accepted.

This was the perfect solution for him, but it complicated our own situation with the newly acquired house on Maxine Lane. We wrote up the agreement and I gave him a check for ten grand. When I got home, I called my lawyer to let him know what I had done. He said, "Well, its non-refundable so there is no way you can get out of it." I said, "that's good, I just don't want him to get out of it!"

Now I had thrown us into a bunch of things; in one month I would have to come up with the cash for the house on Maxine Lane, which needed renovating, and two months later we were going to have to close on the Tulip property, which we really wanted to renovate and move to. I just couldn't take on that much work with my day job at Montgomery and evening/weekend work at Depend-a-Dor!

The only way was to get rid of one property, so I listed Maxine Lane for just over what I was going to have to pay for it. Fortunately it sold and closed at the same time I closed and became the official owner, so it was simply a paper transaction — the net of which was all cash from the sale of the condo that had more than doubled in value.

Tulip was a beautiful house that needed some modernizing but it had good bones. A fabulous 12-foot high rock fireplace supported all the vaulted ceilings in the living room, dining room and kitchen. We put in new floors, kitchen cabinet doors, counter tops and changed all the interior doors and passage sets. All the electrical outlets, switches and light fixtures were upgraded, which made the place look like a new show home.

One rather disturbing experience that occurred while changing the main kitchen light happened just as I removed the old fixture. I was up on the ladder, pulled the light fixture down, and a pile of live ants in a clump the size of a grapefruit came falling out of the electrical box. I had never seen anything like it before. They kept falling as if there was a never-ending supply pouring them out onto the floor from twelve feet up. I got a bucket and put it on the top of the stepladder to catch them while we cleaned up the mess. The next day we got exterminators in and found that there was a huge colony that had made
a home in the 6-inch space between the interior vaulted ceiling and the exterior roof. The reason they had thrived was the stove hood fan vented into that void space instead of directly to the outside, so over the years the grease deposits built up and made a wonderful food source for the ants. One

day Brant called me at work to inform me how so many ants got that far into the house without anyone seeing them. He was on the back deck shooting his Super Soaker water pistol at an army of marching ants, walking single file on top of the clothes line that stretched all the way from the treed back yard to the house. That is where they entered through a crack in the stucco, and once we found their method of access, the problem ended for good.

The Bad Feeling

There was one other problem at Tulip that had a build-up effect on me, which began almost immediately after moving in; it was something that I had never noticed in our other houses. At Hampton Road all the bedrooms were upstairs, so when you got to the top of the stairs you turn right to go to our master bedroom or left to Brant's and a little further down was Shawn's bedroom. I had never thought much about the positioning of their bedrooms and mostly had few reasons to go to their rooms, but the new place was different; our bedroom was at the end of the hall, so I had to pass by their rooms every time I went to ours. That's when I found that we seemed to be raising teen-age pigs! The mess they were comfortable living in was truly depressing, at least for me it was. They also had no concern for saving the planet by energy conservation! Now granted, it was long before the hype of anti-fossil fuels and the global warming paranoia that they would have been currently subjected to; in any event they never turned the lights off. No matter how often I pleaded with them to just not leave everything they own on the floor, and simply turn off their light as they leave for school, nothing worked. Every day when I would come home, I had to pass the entrance to each pigsty, and there, in individual collections, were piles of everything from clothes, shoes, bed sheets, school papers and sports gear in heaps that looked like they were already starting to smolder; and of course, the 100 watt incandescent light bulb shining on it. It was clear I had to take some kind of action that would stop these two boys from doing what I now understand is par for the teen-age course.

I gave them both fair warning that their 'room pits' were going to have to change. The new rule was that anything left on the floor, except shoes of course, would be considered discarded, and I would see to the disposal. Also if a light is left on when they were away, they wouldn't have to remember about flipping a switch off, because they would forfeit their light bulb until the next day.

One would think that a fresh warning would result in some corrective action for at least the first few days, but I was wrong about that too!

The very next day, I came home fully expecting something nice, but no, it was like nothing had been said at all! So I gathered everything that was in contact with the floor, starting with the bed sheet and included pieces of clothing hanging from the open drawers and all the rest of the debris scattered around each room, bundled it like Santa delivering toys, opened the window and tossed each room's contents out their respective window. Then I got the stepladder and removed their light bulbs.

The first day when they discovered their sparse room settings, they seemed genuinely confused and set out looking for their gear until the open window gave them a clue. They didn't appreciate the electrical savings until later that evening.

The next time it happened, which surprisingly, was only a few days later, resulted in some serious groaning. When they asked why I was taking this rather draconian action, I explained that the feeling in their gut that occurred when they looked into their bedroom to find most of it cleared out was the same uncomfortable feeling I got when I had to pass their rooms and see a mess that looked like the remnants of an explosion. I found that over a few weeks, my plan to "cure" the boys was really not very effective and fortunately Marcia came up with a novel solution: close their doors.

Not Just the Water is Cold

After living at Tulip for only two years, we were looking at the possibility of realizing a net tax-free profit of about 60%, so we sold it with the idea of trying something different; moving to a waterfront home on the ocean.

By now, Marcia and I were completely reversing our original structure where she would do all the cooking, to where I was now cooking most of the time. I really liked to cook and she liked that arrangement too. We also thought this might be the time to look at really upgrading our lifestyle, and began looking at expensive waterfront view properties. We decided it would be better to rent rather than buy until we knew exactly what we wanted, so we signed a two-year lease on a townhouse in Cordova Bay that was built literally on the ocean. It straddled the side of the bank with stilts down to the beach, which allowed the ocean to come directly under the deck at high tide. It was a beautiful, modern and sprawling 2,600 square foot two bedroom house plus a den. It had 12-

foot ceilings and the ocean facing walls to the east were mostly glass. Our learning experience started early when we found that the air coming off the water got really cold and seemed to just be looking for a place to trade with something warmer. Well this building had so much glass, along with the newest "radiant heating" system located in the attic. It was supposed to heat objects, not space, but it didn't work, and simply made it difficult to get comfortable. There was a beautiful island cooktop area in the kitchen that was built over the cantilevered area of the house, which straddled the water, but unfortunately when the predominantly cold wind blew in off the ocean it found a way to come into the kitchen. The rather large kitchen had an equally large island counter with a sink and drawers on the food prep side. That is where I could always feel the cold air blowing in from the ocean, right at knee level, so my knees were blue most of the time. We had several small 110-volt space heaters going nearly all the time, and even in summer the decks would be in the shade from 10:00AM on, so it was cold out there all the time. We were not happy with this location and vowed we would never buy based on location without knowing what life is like there first. We were looking forward to the end of our lease when we could move to something more comfortable. Ironically about 6 months before our lease was up, the owners were returning early from living abroad and wanted to move back in as soon as possible. Rather than them having to move into something temporarily, they asked if we would agree to negotiate an early exit. We were pretty happy to get paid to leave.

The Seabird

We loved our time on our 24-foot sailboat but really wanted to get something bigger. We had gone to many boat shows and finally settled on the kind we would look for. Cooper Boatyard in Vancouver had built a Seabird 37, which was a high-end motor sailor with fore and aft cabins each with its own head and shower, extensive use of handcrafted teak on the interior and a 4 cylinder Perkins diesel. Of course I put an ad in the paper, "looking for a Seabird." We got a few responses and over the next few weeks looked at several until we found the one we wanted. I made an offer, which was clearly lower than market for that boat, but we weren't in a hurry. That situation always ensures getting the best deal. The owner thought he could get more by selling it through a broker so I told him to call us for a quick cash sale if he changed his mind. Three months went by and finally we got the call. Shortly thereafter, we were the proud owners of our third Marcia's Den sailboat.

The boat had a teak framed windshield, canvas canopy, and plastic rear window that I wanted to change to a more permanent hardtop. We had also found with our earlier boats, that due to the hassle of rigging and stowing sails, we tended to motor more than sail, so I decided to add a furling mainsail to go along with the furling headsail. The new furling main, which rolled up inside the mast, was all handled from the cabin, so we could have all sails up or down in a few seconds without even going on deck!

This boat had a shoal keel that was only a couple of feet deep and ran the length of the hull which meant we could go into shallow water, however it didn't turn quickly therefore was difficult to maneuver and tack. The hull was very high off the water, which gave us well over six-foot headroom throughout, but any crosswind on the hull would make it very difficult to control when coming into a dock. So I decided to have an 8-inch electric bow thruster installed which meant the boat had to be taken out of the water and into a marine shop, and in order to do that they had to take off the mainmast.

Once it was in the shop, it seemed logical to take that opportunity to replace the teak windshield and canvas with a fiberglass hardtop and glass windows. That is when I decided to have the entire boat painted with two-part epoxy paint.

That paint would permanently eliminate the need to polish the boat in the future. With all this wonderful exterior work making the boat look like it just popped out of its original mold, all it needed was new interior upholstery, so we got that done as well. After three months in the shop and just over $30,000.00, we had the nicest motor-sailor on the West Coast.

When all the work was completed, we were very anxious to get out on it and planned our first trip of the season to Cabbage Island. It was a beautiful sunny day with cruise control engaged, steering a perfect course when only a few miles from the anchorage the wheel started "hunting," which is oversteering in each direction. I thought there was something wrong with the cruise control unit and disengaged it, then found that I had to oversteer in order to maintain a course, so the problem was obviously in the steering system. I thought air must have got into the hydraulic steering unit and because it was getting worse, I planned to bleed the system as soon as we got to anchor. Upon our arrival, though we were the only boat in the bay, we could smell something cooking, probably a BBQ on shore we thought. But there was nobody on shore. Suddenly we realized the cooking smell was coming from our boat! We looked around inside and found nothing but when I lifted the engine room deck plate, a cloud of smoke arose and a fireball flared up. I immediately exhausted a fire extinguisher in the engine space, which knocked the flames down but the smoke kept pouring out. We were only a couple of hundred yards from the beach, so we could easily swim ashore, or cut the dinghy lines from the davits to get away, and let the boat burn to the waterline! Or we could stay and keep trying to get the fire under control.

Had we not just spent all that money on this beautiful boat, our decision would have been easy, but I just couldn't let it go. Marcia was filling a bucket from the galley while I got a portable bilge pump. I jumped into the engine room and sprayed the water bucket where the smoke seemed to be originating from. While Marcia refilled the bucket, I put the pump suction in the bilge and recycled the water back toward the smoke. This went on for a while until I could finally see that the fire was out and the smoke began to dissipate. It turned out that the insulation pad on the engine exhaust manifold gooseneck, which rose to within an inch of the deck head, was a design flaw and that is what caught the underside of the deck on fire. The fire had boiled the hydraulic steering fluid, which explained the steering problems. While underway the fire in the enclosed engine space was starved of oxygen by the engine intake, so when I shut down the engine at anchor, the fire began to take hold, and when I opened the engine space hatch, it virtually exploded.

Once everything was under control, I could see the deck head was half burned through but there seemed to be no other serious problems, and if I could secure some insulation on the manifold, we could take the boat back for repairs. I called Brant, who by now had his own speedboat and asked if he could get a muffler repair kit and bring it out to us. It was sure handy having a 17 year-old kid with his own boat, so we made the temporary repairs and got the boat back for a $9,000.00 insurance claim.

We only had one other problem with the boat over the ten plus years we had it, and that was not due to a design flaw. Marcia and I sailed from CCYC to attend a function at Fidalgo Yacht Club near Anacortes WA. When we arrived the wind was very strong and it was dangerous trying to get tied up, so Marcia was on the front deck with a fender. The wind was blowing so hard I couldn't control the bow even with the bow thruster at full blast. As we were approaching the jetty it looked like we may hit a boat tied there, so Marcia tried to fend us off with her foot, but with a quick snap of the tendons in her knee, found she could not hold back twelve tons of boat. Her knee was a real mess and we realized immediately we would have to go right back to Victoria. I had to stabilize her knee so I wrapped the knee area with cardboard, then took a handle from a deck brush and one from a mop and duct-taped the wooden handles each side of her knee both above and below to splint her leg and we left for Victoria the next morning. The Ocean Current Book showed that the ocean would be running around the back of San Juan Island at up to 8 knots, so we took that route home. It was a beautiful day and our navigation system told us we were travelling at nearly 14 knots over ground! The problem was that as we approached Zero Reef, looking forward we appeared to be heading around it, but we didn't look back to see our trail through the water that showed we were actually being drawn toward it. Marcia was sitting along side me with her leg outstretched when we went right over the reef. It happened so fast we had no chance to take action to avoid it. The boat jumped up about a foot, nearly ejecting Marcia right off the boat, then it heeled over as it groaned across the reef for a few seconds and finally stood upright again! We knew there must be substantial damage and I carefully inspected the lower hull's interior, which fortunately showed no leaks. We also had no prop vibration so we carried on to the Canadian Customs jetty where we already arranged by radio for medical people to meet us and take care of Marcia. When the medics came aboard and saw the splint, they said they couldn't improve on it and took her off to the hospital, broom handles and all! After they left, I headed the boat straight to the drydock and set up a marine survey for the next day. The boat had lost 7 tons of lead shot that poured out through the hole torn in the front of the fiberglass keel. Another expensive insurance repair got the boat back to shipshape and we continued to enjoy our time on board.

Marcia had a long recovery, which still causes her discomfort even after all these years.

Part Six

Ending the Parties:

For nearly twelve years we rented out our ski condo when we weren't using it every other weekend during the season, and it was rarely vacant. By then, we also had five full time residential rentals, so in order to better control our income as well as manage the rentals, we decided to put everything under a management company and incorporated Pinpoint Management Inc.

We managed the ski condo rentals by having a large board with a monthly calendar showing the rental dates and several sets of keys hanging on hooks. Brant had his driver's license and his own car, and secretly planned to take some friends up to party at the mountain. In accordance with a vacancy showing on the board, he took a spare set of keys and arranged to have a sleepover at a friend's house. Some of his friends did the same and they all went up to Mt. Washington. We were surprised when we got a call from the school asking why he wasn't attending, and when the school noted that his friends were also missing, we immediately checked the keys board and found one set gone. After discovering this escapade we re-evaluated our next steps regarding the ski-condo and realized that the market had recovered enough that we could double our money, so it looked like just the right time to sell our original Marcia's Den, and that's what we did.

Graduation:

Shawn was preparing for his high school graduation and was looking for an appropriate wardrobe including a new suit. I was not comfortable with the idea of spending a bunch of money on clothes that would likely only fit for a few months, and on such a fleeting life episode as high school graduation. One evening when we had most of my family over for dinner, including Mom, Dianne, Allan, and Margo, the graduation discussion arose again. In my effort to explain the waste of money that would be regretted in the future, Shawn asked what I wore for my graduation. This was the first time anyone had focused on that time in my life. I stopped, looked at Marcia, then turned to Shawn and said, "I didn't graduate!" Brant and Shawn were the only ones in the room that didn't know. At first they thought I was kidding but when they looked around to the other family members, it was clear, the shocking news was true.

Shawn's new suit fit for several months after his grad, but he didn't get a chance to use it again!

Power Union

When I joined Montgomery Elevator Co. our market share on Vancouver Island was about 40%, and within ten years we were a dominant 60%. We still had strong competition with three other major companies including Otis, but thanks to the single union that controlled all the elevator employees, we ended up getting an additional competitor!

Whenever the market looked like it was headed upward, it meant that developers would be constructing buildings that needed elevators, and that's when the union would start asking for outrageous wages and benefits. It didn't matter that the elevator trade was closed to all but insiders like family and relatives, and they were the highest paid trade in the entire construction industry; they always wanted more and would threaten to go on strike to get it. The union gets its power because they successfully lobbied government to mandate union membership as a requirement to work in BC. So if the only elevator union in BC decides to take away your union membership card, you can no longer work anywhere in the province!

We could not hire anyone that wasn't a union member, and always had to go through the union hall in Vancouver when we needed a mechanic. When we needed to hire someone, even temporarily, we had to take whoever was currently sitting on the bench, and if they happened to be senior, they had the potential to bump a junior, but possibly much better mechanic when cutbacks required us to downsize. With this risk always present, we had to organize spies that would let us know who was next on the bench and determine if it was worth running shorthanded rather than be stuck with a useless senior guy that could endanger one of our junior good guys.

One time when the Plumbers Union was on strike the picketers were outside a strip mall that had escalators serving the second floor, a senior mechanic that worked for Otis Elevator went into the mall to buy something. He was recognized as he left the mall and was reported as a "scab" by a fellow union member to the union hall in Vancouver. He was subsequently summoned to a hearing a few weeks later and got fined $2,000.00. He told them to pound salt and they revoked his union card. He tossed the card at them, stomped out and started his own non-union elevator company. Following that, in spite of great efforts by the union to hurt him, he became a formidable competitor in the trade.

Elevator mechanics lived in constant fear of getting reported for doing more than the union allowed. One example of union tyranny happened to one of our guys that lived near a job site when rather than drive in to our shop to pick up a part that was going to be installed, he took it home and went directly to the job with it the next morning. That cost him $500.00.

The union always seemed ready to protect sub-standard workers. One day the superintendent and I were on our way to a meeting when we saw one of our trucks parked at a mall. On our return about two hours later, the service vehicle was still there. We recognized that our union shop steward operated the truck, but his maintenance route was not in that part of town. When he submitted his time tickets for that day we were able to document that he had falsified his maintenance records. We tried to fire him but the union threatened to strike, so he got a one-week suspension.

One of the worst situations occurred when we were preparing to install new escalators at the Victoria International Airport expansion project. Escalators are a compilation of thousands of very complex moving parts and are assembled on jig tables, aligned with lasers, then shipped from the factory as a complete assembly. Several years earlier the union negotiated a requirement that when escalators arrive from the factory by freight, a local crew must first dismantle them, then re-assemble them prior to installation. This was to compensate for their perceived "loss of local work" as a result of complete factory fabrication! This non-sense affected all the major companies equally so the additional cost was simply added by everyone in the bidding process. The only exception to the "re-assembly requirement" was the one, non-union company that was now even outsourcing escalators. In order to ensure that the company didn't suffer costly problems from mistakes in the re-assembling an escalator in the freight yard, it became routine to pay a crew to take a week off work and then just deliver the untouched equipment to the jobsite for installation. This system worked well for several years until someone complained to the union that they hadn't got their turn for time off.

The business agent from the union came over to confront us on this matter, and though we tried to deny the facts, he went to look at our last installation, where it was clear that the factory paint on the bolts had not been disturbed, so a new union policy was immediately imposed. From that time forward we would be required to dismantle the escalators and before we could re-assemble them, a union agent from Vancouver would have to personally inspect and sign off on the process. All this work is normally completed upon arrival at the freight terminal, which was usually cold, dark and damp, but the new airport terminal expansion promised to be a rare upgrade in working conditions. We had the crated escalators delivered directly to the airport where they had a nice warm well-lit site for us to dismantle the equipment. Shortly after commencing the work, the business agent, who happened to be in town, came by the job. He told our mechanics to stop work, and winch the escalators into the stairwell and then start dismantling them in the enclosed space. Of course that would mean a lot more difficulty and rigging, and add extra days to the installation. When our superintendent saw them dragging the equipment over to the stairwell he told them to stop and do the work in the open. The poor mechanics didn't know what to do. They were too afraid to disobey the union thug, so they carried on dragging the equipment toward the stairwell. They were immediately told to get off the site until we could get this settled. By the time our superintendent got back to our office to let us know about the problem, the union had already taken all our mechanics off their jobs and set up picket lines around every government building our company maintained.

I've never been much of a union supporter, maybe that's why.

Stepping Up Before Stepping Away

I had been promoted a few times over the nearly twelve years since starting with Montgomery. They were mostly name changes because there were only three people in management positions: the General Manager, the technical superintendent, and me in sales / service. A guy at a sales meeting in the USA once gave me good advice: "get regular promotions even if in name only because you can't go from 'Sales' to General Manager, but you can from Sales Manager."

Montgomery Elevator Co., the biggest private elevator company in the world at that time, headquartered in the USA, entered into a joint venture with Kone Corp., a very diversified industrial company from Finland. The plan was to run Montgomery's Canadian elevator operation as Montgomery Kone Elevator Co. I had been with Montgomery for over 10 years and was now the Regional Sales Manager when a General Managers meeting was called in Orlando, Florida. We knew our GM in Victoria was planning to retire sometime soon, and because everyone at the other branches in Canada wanted to get to Victoria, there was a lot of competition for his job. It seemed the inside track would go to our superintendent who was 11 years older than me, and had been with the company for over 20 years. But when it was me that got invited to accompany our GM to the managers meeting in Florida, it was clear they had decided I would be the next head of the branch and General Manager.

Obviously this was difficult for the superintendent, who was also my partner at our overhead door company. Unfortunately things changed in every way from that point on.

When we started Depend-a-Dor we both agreed that we would not make it a family business, as we had seen other companies suffer from the perils that develop from nepotism, especially in a partnership. Problems started when his kids were getting paid to come in on weekends for shop cleaning etc. Working with him was getting more difficult, and now that it was obvious I would soon be his boss at the elevator company. I suggested we sell the door company. He agreed so I started the ball rolling. I got a couple of appraisals and let some accounting firms and commercial realtors know that a viable company was available. When we got a serious enquiry, it was clear that my partner didn't really want to sell, so he came to me one morning and said he wanted to buy me out. I had no problem with that but he wanted to buy my share for about $100,000.00 less than the lowest appraised value. I reminded him about the "shotgun clause" we had in our partnership agreement, which said, if one partner indicates his understanding of the value of the company by way of an offer to the other partner, that partner is automatically entitled to purchase the company at that price!

He also knew I had recently sold a house and had plenty of cash, so I told him to go back and think about it before coming with another offer, and it better not be a discounted price or I'd buy the company from him. I actually didn't want to buy the company and knew he really wanted to keep it and make it a family business.

A few days later he presented an offer that I accepted which included cash plus two of the three warehouses we owned. Unfortunately he had to mortgage his house to pay us out and this led to the complete end of our relationship, which carried over to the elevator company as well. Only months later, I became the GM at Montgomery Kone, but it was a continuous battle, as he never accepted me in that position. It was an unworkable situation but Head Office didn't want to lose either of us, so we were summoned to get on a plane and fly to Toronto to get things settled. They made me several offers, all of which were reasonable, but I found unacceptable. With Marcia's unwavering support, I returned to Victoria, cleared out my desk and left the company.

At the time I was the president of The Victoria Business Exchange, and Vice-president of the Construction Association of Victoria. I was in my early 40's, we had plenty of cash, no debt and owned several rental properties; I figured I could carry on in business and work at something else if I wanted, but I decided to retire.

If You Can, You Can't

I had always thought that "the first guy to retire wins," and shortcuts should get you there faster, but now I was in for a few new life lessons. After about three or four months of doing nothing, I found myself watching Oprah in the afternoons! This was a very scary situation for a guy who was used to working two or three jobs at the same time, and now was doing nothing all day! What if I lived to be 60?! I hadn't considered this level of boredom because I was always too busy to get used to sitting around and I hadn't developed any other interests or diversions that could help pass the time. I was never a soloist because I enjoyed doing things with other people, now I found that I was alone because all my friends were working. It was a painful way to learn that if you can get yourself into a position where you can retire early and do nothing for the rest of your life, you soon find that you are not the kind of person that is comfortable doing nothing. Conversely, if you are the kind of person that would be comfortable doing nothing while you are relatively young, you will never get into the position of early retirement! I had golfed once or twice a year in the typical company golf tournaments, but always dismissed the game because it took up too much valuable time. Now, just as it began to look like a more sensible thing to do, I got a call from my old boss from the Mount Washington Ski Resort project.

I hadn't had much contact with Knute Johnson since I had left for Montgomery some 12 years earlier, but we were very good friends, and he had heard through the Construction Association that I had recently retired. He was twenty years older than me, had just retired himself, and now found himself in a similar boring predicament. He called and asked if I was interested in taking up golf! We started a new chapter in our lives as we took up the game. We really enjoyed our time together and Knute was very interested in travelling to various locations in the U.S. with golf as the focal point.

I found that this game could be quite expensive so I decided to try and make it pay! I started a Pinpoint Management subsidiary company called Golf-2-Go that I intended to use as a golf travel business. I found in trying to organize my first trip to Laughlin NV that it was impossible to make money without the economy of scale, and with only about 5 others that signed up, it was just not workable. I cancelled the group trip and just Knute and I went. After that trip I thought of another way to make Golf-2-Go work. I contacted golf courses in Palm Springs and Phoenix and setting up a "visit to evaluate" their golf course. The idea was to evaluate the golf courses from an ordinary or average golfer's perspective and set up special rates for large building complexes in the surrounding area. I had monogrammed shirts and hats, designed evaluation forms, created a website and communicated in advance via fax to set up the complimentary rounds. It was a lot of work because I had to coordinate playing on successive days in each location in order to justify the cost of the trip, but we got to play many of the best courses in the southwest U.S. for free. Knute joined me on numerous golf trips and travel adventures; we had many great times until his death nearly twenty years later.

More Opportunities

Though I was playing a lot of golf, I was still very much under-utilizing my spare time, when my brother Mark in Toronto called. Mark was a natural executive type. Before he was twenty years old he parlayed his way into a management position with the Hudson Bay store in Regina, then became an executive with Sask Oil and was now the vice-president of Knowell Therapeutics, a Toronto based company that provided an anti-cavity solution for dental office applications. They needed someone to do seminars for dentists in various cities as well as in-office training sessions. It seemed well outside my skill set, but Mark was convinced I was the guy they needed. After a lot of discussion, I thought I'd give it a try. I had to read hundreds of dental publications, research papers and studies, but soon I became an expert in a very specific area of dental microbiology.

This was a very interesting and challenging new direction in my life that required me to travel all over western Canada putting on seminars for dentists. The focus of my work was to teach dentists a new form of preventive technology that had been developed at the University of Toronto Faculty of Dentistry. Typically I would do two or three evening seminars a month for 10 to 15 dentists at each location. It was really fun because I was a kind of "rock star" that would show up for all these dentists who had paid over $300.00 each to attend. The venues were organized by the head office in Toronto and they also provided a roadie person who would drive a van full of presentation materials to the hotel, get all the setup completed, and I would fly in to do the presentation. I was an independent contractor so I had a great deal of autonomy, and because I wasn't a dentist, I always had a dentist paid to come with me to each presentation, so when questions veered from my level of expertise I could call on him to handle those specifics. Over time the company became Oralife and the focus changed from teaching the procedure to getting the procedure covered by corporate dental benefits programs. My presentations shifted from dealing with the dental providers to the HR departments of major companies and union organizations.

During this time I was recognized by the Faculty of Dentistry as an expert in this specific area of dental microbiology, and became accredited to teach at the dental schools. Dentists are required to take a certain number of credit courses each year, and because I was qualified to teach them, we had great times with several of my dentist friends when I scheduled some courses at ski resorts!

As a result of my involvement with the College of Dental Surgeons of BC, I was approached by First Canadian Health Corp., a major dental plan payer of reimbursement of dental procedures throughout Canada. They asked me if I would entertain being a dental auditor for them. This meant I would schedule a one, two or three day visit to selected dental offices all over the country and verify the reimbursement details with their dental procedure records. I took that job because again, I was not an employee, but it gave me even more freedom to schedule audits where they wanted me to go, but also when I wanted to go. I only did about two or three audits a month and was very well paid for each; however I found that line of work very boring, so after a year or so, I decided to retire again.

When I was with Montgomery and owned Depend-a-Dor, I was always in charge of accounts receivable and made sure we collected all outstanding accounts. This included several successful Small Claims Court challenges. My habit of looking for the shortcut never applied in these situations; the main reason I always won is because I put more effort in collecting than they expected.

One collection case that stands out in my mind was a hotel that had not paid its elevator maintenance bills for several months. They always had some excuse, but the outstanding bills kept increasing until I realized that we would not be able to salvage the business relationship anymore, so I gave them an ultimatum: pay or we'd be going to court.

It quickly became obvious that they had been through this routine before, and made no effort to mitigate the situation. I filed a claim in Small Claims Court, and was a little surprised when they filed a response to dispute the claim! They were headquartered in Vancouver but we ended up in court on Vancouver Island where the hotel was located, which added to their cost and inconvenience. They tried to argue the validity of the Maintenance Agreement as a rationale for not paying for the services we had rendered. It was a rather foolish gambit, as I knew every word and the meaning of every phrase in the agreement; after all, I had been selling that agreement for years. I won a judgment for the full amount plus costs and interest, which now was nearly double the original debt. It seemed the hotel never had any intent to pay, with or without a court judgment, and they set out to show me just how hard it would be to collect any money.

They greatly underestimated my resolve and experience in this field. I always took this kind of thing personally. It came down to a basic competition; someone was going to win and someone was going to lose. I was in the right in this fight, so the loser wasn't going to be me!

I went to the BC Companies Office to look at their documents to see where I could go after some of their assets, but found that they had protected themselves from creditors by placing a chattel mortgage on every asset in the hotel, even including the chairs in the pub and dishes in the restaurant!

I was very discouraged at first and thought they might beat me, but then I came up with a plan. I knew that the pub was always busy on weekends and I figured they must stock up on liquor prior to Friday nights. I went to the Sheriff's office with my Court Order, paid nearly $2000.00 for their services in advance, and asked that they go in to the hotel pub on Friday at approximately 6:00PM. I told them the pub would have several thousand dollars in liquor and beer kegs and they should ask for full payment including the newly added Sheriff's fees, or seize every ounce of liquor on the premises.

When the Sheriff arrived and confronted the bartender he had no idea what to do, so he called the owner in Vancouver and explained the situation. That's when the owner realized he was not going to win this one, and authorized full payment. Ironically the bar manager didn't have enough cash on hand to satisfy the order, so the owner had to give the manager the code for a special safe that contained additional cash. The hotel ended up paying nearly three times the original cost, but we got paid in full.

Collecting on outstanding debt was always a problem even with a court order. One of the most unusual cases I experienced was when I got a judgment against a very large development company that had not paid for the elevator installation on a construction project. We had recently completed some work on site and shortly thereafter the company went into receivership. This is similar to bankruptcy but in this case an accounting firm takes over the operation and continues to operate the company while looking to sell the company and or its assets. Once a company goes into receivership, all company assets are frozen, and all creditors are held away from any further collection actions. Also the creditors are divided into two groups: secured and non-secured. Secured creditors like banks are those that have a mortgage or chattel on the project or the company's assets and they get paid first; anything left goes to the non-secured creditors. Usually after the receiver is paid, then the secured creditors take their share, there is nothing left for the other supplier companies and the trades.

I had started the Small Claims action before the company went into receivership, and they didn't respond so I subsequently got a default judgment, which could not have occurred after the receivership commenced. I went to the BC Companies office again to look at the company assets and found they had nearly a dozen company vehicles including large trucks, pickups, vans as well as two nearly new luxury cars, a Lincoln and a Cadillac. I presumed the CEO and the VP used the fancy cars for their personal transportation. When the receiver informed us that we were included as a non-secured creditor, I enquired what assets were seized at their corporate office and construction yard. They listed the assets and vehicles I had noted in my earlier investigation, however neither of the two luxury cars were included in the impound list. I suspected that when the receiver took possession of the assets on their premises, the cars were at the executive's homes and therefore were overlooked.

I went to the Sheriff's office with the judgment, paid their exorbitant fee in advance, and gave them the addresses of both executives, saying they would find a Lincoln or a Cadillac at their residences and they should ask for full payment or have the vehicles towed and impounded. The Sheriff had done this kind of collection many times in the past and knew the best time to show up was at 6:30 AM with a tow truck. The Sheriff did exactly that. The first house had the Lincoln, so he got the tow operator to hook up and then knocked on the door. This was the VP's residence and he was shocked to see the action in his yard. He was given the option to pay several thousand in cash or surrender the vehicle for auction. He paid and they left him with the car. I think both vehicles ended up in the hands of the executives because the receiver had missed them, so they were never included in the company assets. We got paid in full for our claim and about a year and a half later; we got a payment for "final settlement of the receivership," as a non-secured creditor, in the amount of $17.00!

One time our accountant phoned Marcia, because she did the books for our door company, asking why she had not put any reserve dollar figure for account write-offs. She told him that I was in charge of collecting all the accounts receivable and there were no write-offs! The accountant was shocked because he had never seen a service company with no bad debt write-offs.

From my past business experience I knew that most businesses had trouble with their accounts receivables, and they would gladly welcome help collecting, so it made sense that was my next direction. I called the new company The Accounts Doctor, a subsidiary to Pinpoint Management Inc. The motto on my business card was, "We'll take the pains out of your arrears." Shortly after distributing a few cards around town, I started getting calls for help with their delinquent accounts. The first company to call me for an appointment was a large successful music company. They wanted to try me out by seeing if I could retrieve an entire drum set that a member of a band had rented over a year earlier and subsequently skipped. Every effort they had made so far had proven fruitless. I took their information and told them I'd be back. I called one of the numbers they had on the file for the guy that had the drum set but the person that answered the phone said that guy didn't live there anymore. I told him that I had found a drum cover bag with his name on it and wondered if he knew where the guy was living now. He gave me the information I needed, so I decided to go to see the drummer at a time I figured he would likely be home; about 6:30 PM. I also didn't know if I would be encountering him surrounded by his band buddies, so I asked my son Shawn to

come with me. Shawn is bigger than me, and I'm not small. He has extensive experience in 'mixed martial arts' and is former professional bouncer. So when I rang the doorbell, with Shawn standing slightly behind me, the woman quickly called the guy to the door. When he appeared, I used the old sales technique called the "alternate close." This is where you only offer two choices, and both lead to the end result you intend
to achieve. I said, "I'm here to get the drum set. Do you want us to come in and get them or would you prefer to bring them out here where we can load them in the truck?" He simply said, "I'll get them."

The next day I showed up at the music store and asked where they wanted me to drop off the drum set? Needless to say they were blown away with my initial performance and immediately became a regular client.

Over time I got very tired of constantly dealing with people with financial troubles and especially those who just wanted to rip off the company they owed money to, so I wound down my activities in collections.

Cameo

We had booked a sailing trip in the British Virgin Islands with another couple on a 42-foot Hunter sloop nearly a year in advance, however I had just left Montgomery Kone, so we considered canceling, but decided to go anyway. It was a fabulous experience. We met another couple in the BVI's on an identical boat, and found they had chartered from the same company! I commented how expensive it is for two couples to charter a boat but was surprised to find this young single couple got theirs for much less than half of what we had paid!

The most expensive way to charter is to book it a long time in advance; the cheapest is to be available for a last minute opportunity, when they will discount heavily in order to get some revenue and avoid a vacancy. It was a very unique experience but considering we already owned a beautiful 37-foot boat, it seemed a little extravagant.

As we contemplated leaving our leased waterfront townhouse in Cordova Bay I was on the lookout to purchase a house, and found one on Cameo St. that had very good bones as well as development potential. We bought it and immediately renovated it with a new kitchen, solid oak floors and built a 2-bedroom suite in the basement with a ground level entrance.

During our transition to this house Brant and Juliana got married on March 25, 1995 in a beautiful ceremony at Chrystal Gardens.

Marcia Gives Even More

Shortly after Brant and Juli's wedding Marcia took the full time position as service coordinator with Accutemp Refrigeration. She had done all the bookkeeping and shared in the day-to-day office management duties at our door company for the nearly ten years we owned it, and up until the wedding had been working for a temporary employment agency. The refrigeration company operation was very similar to our door company, in having to provide maintenance and emergency repairs as well as installations, so after only three years Marcia became the office manager and oversaw the operational dispatch of the mechanics.

One day she received a request from her oldest brother Tony, as did her other thirteen siblings, asking if anyone would consider donating a kidney! Tony had been a diabetic since his teens and his health had degenerated to the point that he was going to be on dialysis three days a week for the foreseeable future, and his future was not extending out very far. For various reasons Marcia was the only candidate in the family that was able to successfully go through the extensive medical selection and elimination process. She made arrangements to carry on with the kidney donation in Saskatoon. The surgery was a complete success except for Marcia having a rib removed that caused pain for years after; Tony got a new lease on life and he and his family celebrate their gratitude for Marcia's incredible gift every year on the anniversary.

Part Seven

The Dreaded Restaurant

At 18 years old, while still using crutches following a life threatening motorcycle accident, Brant decided to start an upscale pool hall that included a kitchen for light lunches and snacks. It became quite successful so Brant sold it, paid back his early financial supporters with a healthy return, and started another larger version, again from scratch, but much closer to downtown called The Bridge St. Billiard Cafe. One of the investors in his first venture was a developer who had recently bought a multiple unit housing project that surrounded a small strip mall in Regina. Knowing what Brant had done before, he called from Regina and suggested Brant come out to look at a derelict restaurant in a strip mall next to the developer's new project. Brant flew out and returned with video showing me the "incredible value." The stainless kitchen alone, with all the equipment would have been over $200K, and though the land was on a long-term lease, we could own the entire building for a couple of hundred grand! We just had to put up $80K! If Brant got a mortgage for the rest, it could work. Marcia was quite skeptical about getting involved in this notoriously risky business. I knew she was right, but I also knew that if we didn't put up the money, all possibilities would die on the spot and that might be a great opportunity lost. We decided to go ahead with the project, Brant got the mortgage, and then he, Juliana and Shawn packed up and headed for Saskatchewan.

They named it The Dizzy Monk. It was a huge undertaking and over the next two years everyone involved would learn a lot. Brant learned how difficult it is to run a six thousand square foot, double bar operation. The bar and kitchen staff were constantly engaged in various forms of theft while Brant was busy coordinating live entertainment and dealing with the financials. The job was a daunting, seven days a week task and in the end the main thing we learned was that in spite of the fact that we owned the building and had a 30-year lease on the land that our building sat on, the owner of the strip mall could make it impossible to survive. What we didn't know, was that due to the close proximity of our location to the university, the landowner had entered into talks with a large fast food chain, which would suit the location much better than a sports bar. If the mall owner could squeeze us out, they could acquire the building free and get a much higher rent. So the (land owner) company began a barrage of outrageous requests for us to undertake, as the building owner, including repainting the building and replacing the roof. The mall owner was a very large corporation with in-house lawyers, so they had no problem backing every unrealistic demand with court action threats and sheriff summons deliveries. Eventually when it was clear we could not survive, I flew out to Regina to make a final decision on winding-down the venture. Brant went to the mortgage company and told them what was happening and that we could not continue. The bank was going to be on the hook for nearly $200K, and realized that if Brant wasn't going to be there to operate the bar, it would be a total loss, so they said they would meet with the mall owner and work out some kind of deal. Following their meeting, they contacted Brant and said they saw exactly what the company had been doing to him and they were going to take over the fight. They said they would discharge Brant from the mortgage free and clear! The bank was so disgusted with the company that they planned to undertake action to move the building rather than give it to the predator mall owner. Brant was allowed to just walk away and the bank did eventually sell the building to a brewpub operation. Brant, Juliana and Shawn moved back to Victoria and the brewpub had the entire building moved to a property they owned on the other end of town, where it is still in operation today!

I guess one could say Marcia and I lost our two son's education fund on this adventure, but in reality it was the tuition we paid to the school of hard knocks, for another form of education. I now think that money did as much good for them as any other kind of school.

Dreary Winters

The year after we chartered the sailboat in the BVIs a friend who was the president of the Construction Association of Victoria asked if Marcia and I would like to rent an RV and join him and his wife as they were planning a winter trip in the USA in their motorhome. We thought that would be great and organized a rental for us to pick up in Nashville, TN in late January. Our friends were waiting for us at the airport; we stayed with them the first night and headed for the RV center the next day to pick up our coach. It was a "C" class motor home that was brand new. Normally that would be a good thing, but this unit had never been tested to make sure it had everything one would need and that everything worked. Well we certainly found all the shortcomings of this unit. One of the drawer catches didn't work, and of course it was the drawer that contained all the cutlery, so as we drove around the first corner, the drawer came flying out with a startling crash and emptied the cutlery all over the floor. The dining table, which was normally stored away for more living space by hanging on a hinged side, had a support leg that was too short, so when we sat at the table, it was on a 15-degree angle. We found out later that the flexible hose for emptying the sewage-holding tank was supposed to have a hard 90-degree elbow to hold it in the dump tank at the campsite. I had no experience in this area so I just put the flexible hose in the tank opening, but when I opened the valve on the RV, the sewage came rushing down the 3-inch hose and as soon as it hit the turn down to the tank, it jumped out and sprayed raw sewage all over the ground around the site. We weren't impressed with this unit but we thought the RV concept had merit.

The following year, it was mid-February and I was driving back to Victoria in pouring rain from an exceptionally boring three-day audit of a dental office in Nanaimo when I realized I needed to make another major change. I suffer from Seasonal Affective Disorder (SAD), that means I need to have a lot of natural light from the sun, or I become depressed, which is why we moved to the townhouse on the water with ten-foot high glass windows, but here I was in

Victoria, in the winter, driving in the rain after doing a job I didn't really like!

I started thinking, I haven't planned this out very well, and I'm going to change that. About the time I came up with the idea that I would buy an RV and get away from these grey skies next year, I saw a sign on the road at Cobble Hill saying "Come in to see our line of RVs!" I immediately pulled in and started walking around. I think I was the only customer they had seen since late August and I had already figured that negotiating advantage. I found a fifth-wheel I liked and said, "I have never owned an RV and don't even own a truck to pull this thing, but I'm prepared to buy this one and I'll write a check now, but here is my price." It was a terrible offer, but I wasn't in a rush and knew I'd find something over the next few months, but to them it meant "cash!" This probably represented their first bit of potential revenue since last summer, so after many efforts to get me to raise my price, they finally conceded and accepted my low-ball offer. Part of the offer included that they deliver our next "Marcia's Den" to our house in Victoria. Shortly thereafter we ordered a brand new custom truck all fitted with a tow package to pull our new toy. Being an auditor was far too boring for me, so I quit doing audits; Marcia left the AC company and that was the last winter spent in Victoria.

From Sail to Boathouse

We were now going to California and Arizona in our RV in the winter and still had our beautiful 37' sailboat parked at CCYC for summer fun, but having a boat worth over $100K sitting exposed and not maintained for about half the year began to make less and less sense. So we decided to sell that Marcia's Den and look at a smaller powerboat that we could put it in a boathouse. We were happy to sell it for over $80K, which meant that the capitol cost was about $1000.00/year over the entire time we had it, and that's pretty good! We bought a fully renovated 27-foot Bayliner Sunbridge that was called "Cool Change." The name was so appropriate that we didn't re-name it. It had an inboard/outboard with a separate aft cabin located below the cockpit, and because of our seniority in the yacht club, we were able to get a boathouse immediately.

Crash to the Party:

Mark and Allan were in Victoria for one of our annual O'Boys excursions, in this case, a boat trip to one of the Gulf Islands aboard my first powerboat Cool Change. The plan was to tie up at Pender Island and play a round of golf at a course that we knew was accessible by walking from the harbor. When we arrived the wind was really howling and the only way to safely get to the dock was to go past it down wind and go astern straight back to the jetty. I had to give the astern plenty of throttle in order to offset the wind, and everything seemed to be going according to plan until we got close and I tried to slow down. The single cable for engaging the transmission and throttle broke, which sent us stern first, at speed, right into the jetty! The swim grid hit first, crushing it until the jetty hit the next line of defense, which was the dinghy mounted on its side across the stern of the boat. It smashed the dinghy and sent the mounting brackets through the stern of the boat. What a way to start our little golf get-away boat trip! Once we got the boat tied up, I did a thorough inspection of the rear sections of the boat to see if there was any danger of it sinking. Fortunately all the damage was above the waterline. I immediately called my insurance agent and told him about the mishap. He said he'd send a tow boat out the next morning, so when I got off the radio telephone, I told the boys to get the golf clubs out, "We're going golfing!"

The next morning a towboat showed up and the pilot told us we would not have to do anything, he would get us back. So he hooked us up, and we went below, put on a spectacular breakfast and enjoyed a carefree trip back from inside.

In the old days, I loved to go out to the boat and tinker, without even taking it out on the water, but now I liked the idea of having the boat sit unattended in the boathouse for the entire winter and even weeks at a time in the summer!

We were actually done with boating, but hadn't admitted it to ourselves yet. That realization occurred when I got a call from the club director of moorage, telling me that otters got on the boat and seemed to have had a party on the rear deck. I can tell you that otters do not have clean parties, and the stink they leave behind quickly resembles a skunk. So there we were in California and he tells us we have to get this mess cleaned up, and quickly before the smell permeates the wood in the boathouse. We had to coordinate that project from long distance, and soon realized it was time for us to move on from boating; we sold it and haven't missed boating since, but we have maintained our CCYC membership, just in case!

Making Good on a Leaky Problem

In the mid 90's certain changes in the building code resulted in a catastrophic effect on many condo complexes called The Leaky Condo Syndrome. This is where the structural studs in the building would rot behind the stucco exterior requiring major, expensive refitting to fix the problem. As a result of this plague that swept the condo market, primarily on the West Coast where wet conditions are more prevalent, condo prices dropped dramatically. Financial institutions also tightened up their lending criteria. In fact it became nearly impossible to secure a mortgage on a condo. With a flood of people finding they couldn't afford the repair cost, and at the same time the market value had dropped by more than 50%, and thus wiping out any equity they had, most people just walked away.

I recognized that there was great value in the depressed condo market, because there was increasing competition to get rid of these doomed units and few people in a position to acquire them. I called a realtor and asked him to find a condo that was in foreclosure, where I knew I could deal directly with the bank. He quickly found several that had 2 bedrooms, 2 full bathrooms, six appliances and secure underground parking, which had originally sold new for nearly $170K. They were now offered by the bank at less than half the original price, but because they were in foreclosure, every sale had to go through the court process. I told the realtor to go to court with my offer of $75,000.00, and explained that I would not increase my offer, because I didn't care if it was successful or not. A week or so later, he came back with a signed agreement, but impressed upon me that there were investors at court that would be making it more difficult to get deals like this in the future. I decided to go to court with the realtor to buy another one. As it turned out there were three other investors at court wanting to buy units, so when three offers were presented for one unit, the judge asked each of the investors to go out in the hall and submit a final "sealed bid offer." I went out to the hall and gathered the three investors, told them that there were several units available, and I would pay them each $1000.00 cash immediately not to submit a bid on this particular unit. They agreed, I submitted the only bid of $5000.00 less than the previous offers, and got the condo. I eventually bought four condos out of receivership averaging about $65K each, but as a result of my hallway antics, the court recognized its procedural errors and permanently changed their method of dealing with multiple receivership bids.

Call of the U.S.

When Brant and Juliana moved back from Regina, they moved into the two-bedroom suite on the lower level of our house on Cameo, and shortly thereafter their son Kahless was born. Brant was restless and wanted to get into some form of media, like movies or TV, so he dreamed up a kind of pilot for a TV show called Party Quest. It involved organizing young adults to compete in various types of physical bar games in cities across Canada. It required a tremendous amount of advance coordination but with the help of his brother Shawn and nearly a dozen core people; they took a fully decaled bus filled with camera, sound, and production crews from Victoria to Newfoundland. Two winners, a girl and boy were chosen from each city to go to Mexico and compete in the final contest. Brant arranged for this all to occur at a five star resort in Cancun. The group of about 60 people, including contestants and crews for production and filming all headed to Mexico. Brant asked if I wanted to come and watch the action, but remembering my Mexican 'throat-cutting' lesson from so many years ago, I declined — however when Brant sent me the tickets to fly to Cancun and stay a week in an all expenses paid, all-inclusive, five star resort I couldn't resist.

It was very impressive watching Brant handle this project. When he returned, I accompanied him to the National Association of Television Production Executives (NATPE) convention in Los Vegas where eventually things lead to him getting the attention of David Foster, the famous multi-Grammy winning record producer in Los Angeles. He and David became instant friends and David let Brant live at his house in Malibu for a few weeks while David put Brant in touch with some key people in the TV business. Soon Brant was approached by a production company and got an all expenses paid move for he and his family to Los Angeles. His first TV show called The Princes of Malibu was shot at David's house where Brant was in charge of a production crew of nearly two hundred people.

Shortly after moving to the U.S., Brant and Juliana had their second child, a girl and our first American grandchild, Briana.

Drifting Apart

Marcia had been very busy with directing her Sweet Adelines chorus and was often out of town teaching or judging at competitions so I found it was difficult to coordinate getting away for the winter in our new RV rig. I knew our boating opportunities in previous summers had always been dictated by Marcia's travel schedule or weekly chorus commitments, and now I felt our winter travel was running up against similar restrictions. We went to southern California with the RV and traveled through many of the beach cities, but Marcia had to go to her events so I decided to carry on in the RV alone. Two of my dentist friends flew down to Mesa AZ to join me in the RV for a few days and while they were there, we bought a house! We were already partners in an apartment block and other real estate ventures in Victoria, so it was no big deal to add another asset. We threw in a low-ball offer that was surprisingly accepted without a counter. It was a simple 1960's two-bedroom bungalow that needed complete upgrading, so we paid cash for it and planned that I would do all the renovations. In the mean time, I left the RV in the driveway and flew back to Victoria to confront another issue.

Marcia and I had slowly been drifting apart and although we never fought, I felt like we had been living separate lives so I decided we should separate. There were many loose ends to deal with because we had several rental properties and many other assets to divide. I was 52 and didn't know at the time that I was in a serious midlife crisis. This was the beginning of me making a sequence of bad decisions.

Marcia moved out of the house on Cameo to a basement suite at a friend's house. The lower level suit at Cameo was already rented following Brant and Juliana's move to LA, so I got the upper level rented and flew back to Phoenix to complete the renovations. It was an opportunity for me to escape in many ways, and I worked seven days a week for just over a month getting the place fully modernized. When the renovations were completed, I towed the RV back to Victoria and found an apartment to live in.

The grey and lonely time in Victoria gave me plenty of occasions to reflect on "what was I doing?"

I found my feelings were quite close to the surface and though I had always been able to function on my own, this was very different. The next six or seven months when we were separated went very slowly. There were times when we would meet to see our grandson when they came up for a visit. Then Mark and Gerri came from Florida for a few days and Marcia unexpectedly joined us at a pub. This upheaval in our lives made Marcia literally sick over the six plus months, but when she unexpectedly walked in to the pub, all eyes turned to her, and she was stunning. It was only days later that we thought we'd try getting together for a 'date?' By then I was certainly ready to come to my senses. It was like a new love in our lives, only better, so we agreed to get back together.

Marcia moved in with me on the waterfront in a beautiful 2-bedroom south-facing apartment overlooking the Victoria harbor.

We thought it would be nice to have a party. Our 33rd wedding anniversary was coming up, so in April of 2004 we held a big party for all our family, relatives and friends at the yacht club (CCYC) where we also renewed our wedding vows and I read my poem:

When I reflect upon our life together
it seems we had mostly favorable weather.
Your endless support and boundless love
was the wind that helped us to sail above.

When I gaze at the young kind of man I was
always the cause of some action or buzz.
But your quiet stable and steady hand
kept at least one of my feet in touch with land.

When I think of things that make me proud
it was you that kept my eyes from cloud.
Not that I have accomplished so very much
but all that I have bears your velvet touch.

When I see the storm I steered toward
blind of the perils for all aboard.
I now see the fog that I couldn't see
and feel your spirit that reguided me.

When I consider my flounder with midlife's force
your love and commitment held the true course.

What could have ended our family and fate
has brought me back to my only soul mate.

When I look back on all our years
I am happy to say even through the tears.
You were always the only one for me
and I promise that's the way it will always be.

Part Eight

A New Construction Project

A few weeks after the big party, we set out on our first new adventure together; a construction project in Port Alberni. I met an old friend from the Construction Assoc. that had built a townhouse development, and due to sagging market conditions, he wanted to redesign the stand-alone unused recreation center into a two-bedroom residential condo.

We made a deal that gave me a comfortable budget where I could do as much of the work as I wanted, but there was a bonus time clause. If I finished early, every day added to the bonus, and conversely every day I was late in completion would add to a financial penalty. Marcia and I took our RV to the site on Cherry Creek Road and set it up beside the building that would soon be someone's residence. Marcia and I had done many renovations in the past so we really enjoyed this lucrative opportunity to work together.

It was a big project that involved breaking out the concrete floor for plumbing, knocking out walls and installing windows, walls, an extra bathroom and new kitchen. We worked well together and got a lot done over long hot days. At the end of every day, we would hop in the truck and head over to the crystal clear river and have a refreshing swim. We got to the point where I had all the rough-in and framing complete, and just had the mountain of drywall delivered. Working with 12-foot sheets is not pleasant, so I called a few drywall companies and happened to catch one that had just finished a job that day. The guy came by in a few minutes and took some measurements, gave me a quote and said they could start in an hour! Knowing that this would dramatically cut my completion time, and since I really disliked installing drywall anyway, I agreed. This guy, who was a really big dude, probably at least 6 foot 6, immediately pulled out his phone and called his crew to our location, he then put some screws in his mouth, grabbed a 12 foot sheet of drywall, held it on the wall with one hand and a knee then screwed it in place! He had more than half a dozen sheets in place, including cutouts for electrical boxes before the crew showed up! These guys worked like a machine and had the entire 2-bedroom condo boarded in just over two days! The rest of the project went just as well and we finished all the construction a week early.

The New Big Rig

We had spent a few winters in the LA area in our RV and knew this was going to be our routine for the foreseeable future, but the idea of making it more comfortable in a bigger RV was quite prevalent, so whenever there was an RV show we went out of our way to go see the new features available in the bigger units. At one show, west of LA, we stumbled upon what we thought would be our perfect 5th wheel, which also meant we would need a new truck to pull it. It was January and we were already comfortably set up in Castaic CA near Brant and Juli's house, so getting a new truck and RV in the U.S. would involve a lot of complicated paperwork and inconvenience due to the fact that we were Canadians in the U.S. with a BC registered RV and truck.

But I thought if I could find a dealer in Washington State near the Canadian border that carried the model of RV we wanted, I could work out a deal for March when we would be in the area, on our way back. Thanks to the internet, I found a dealer in Mount Vernon, WA and he had three new units in stock, including the interior color package we wanted; however they were covered with snow. This condition was reminiscent of the first RV we bought! So over the phone I told the salesman we wouldn't be at his location until March and if he would accept my one-time, non-negotiable, low offer, as well as keep the unit insured on his lot until we arrived, I would send him full payment the next day. Again my offer represented the only cash flow his dealership would have seen, or would see in months, so after much consideration, he accepted, and I sent the money. Our next priority was to find a suitable truck to pull the rig. Through the miracle of the internet, I was able to find the perfect truck; a Ram 3500 diesel short box, crew cab, at a dealer in Maple Ridge, BC. I worked out a deal where they would keep the truck insured on their lot until March. A few months later we were excited to see our new RV at the dealer in Washington State where we completed the paperwork and told him we would go up to Vancouver, drop our current RV and return to pick up the new one. Our gas-powered truck could pull the new RV empty so it was no problem getting it up to the RV site in the Vancouver area where we parked it right beside our old unit. While Marcia began to transfer our stuff from the old RV to the new one, I drove to Maple Ridge to get our new truck. They asked me to bring the old rig in to them because they get many requests for smaller, matched truck and 5th wheel rigs. The next day they made me a cash offer I couldn't refuse! They gave me a ride back to the RV park where our new truck and RV where waiting to be taken home to Victoria.

The Start and End of Touring

We loved the new RV that we never used in the summer while we were in Victoria, but was a great home for us in California. We didn't have much interest in touring because we liked being set up near Brant and Juliana especially since she was pregnant with their third kid which would be our second American-born grandkid. Marcia was available to drive Juliana to the hospital for the birth of our second grandson, Braden, whose name is a combination of Brant/Dennis. That season, we spent nearly every day at their house.

Brant had purchased a residential building lot right next door to their current house and began the project of building a new palace, even bigger than the 4000+ square foot house they were living in. Marcia was helping Juli with the two kids and now a new baby that kept them well occupied. My construction experience was valuable as Brant was busy in TV work and I was there to deal with the general contracting issues. It turned out to be nearly seven days a week for the entire winter. When we headed for Victoria there was still well over a thousand square feet that was destined to be a billiard room and theater, which was to be completed in my absence.

When we came back in October, we were surprised to find that little had been done, so that's when we decided to go touring in our 5th wheel. Starting in San Diego we stopped at most of the RV parks for a week or so making a loop through Escondido, Oceanside, Temecula and planned to stop in Hemet, Lake Elsinore, and Perris. When we got to Hemet, a town with one main street that feels very small, but has everything the large centers have, we ended up staying a couple of months! I was playing golf at Seven Hills Golf Course, one of the two courses located within the city perimeter, and happened to see a "for sale" sign on a good looking house along the 9th fairway, so I called the phone number, between golf shots, and set in motion a course of action that would significantly change our lives again.

The real estate market across the entire U.S. was in a sharp decline because of faulty federal government policies, which had helped very unqualified people get into home ownership.

Unqualified borrowers could not meet their requirements and had to sell or walk away. When the real estate market became flooded with people trying to bail out, it caused the market to crash even further, more people found themselves "up-side down" because all their equity had evaporated and they now owed far more than the value of their property, so most of them just walked.

This is what led to one of the biggest financial disasters and real estate market crashes in the world.

Timing Is Everything

When everything came crashing down, nobody could get money. Banks were no longer lending to people who couldn't afford a loan, and they weren't even lending to people who could! I could always recognize an opportunity, so it looked like just the right time to buy a house in the U.S. Unfortunately there was still a substantial difference in the U.S. / CDN dollar. If I purchased an average house for cash it would cost at least an additional $30,000.00 just for the exchange. I tried to get a U.S. mortgage so I wouldn't have to pay that exchange premium and though we had the cash in our Canadian bank and a letter of unconditional credit from our bank stating the bank would guarantee payment of up to half a million dollars, we could not get a mortgage. Of course these conditions exacerbated the decline in house prices. The market crash was nearing full bloom about the time we got to Hemet in our RV.

That is when I made the call from the 9th fairway of Seven Hills Golf Course and made an appointment. We went to see the house and fortunately for us the beneficiaries of the estate had left it in a disgusting state of disarray. The price had already been reduced about six times, but the house had good bones and was located in a lovely little gated community called East Lake that was obviously well managed. We made what I thought was a ridiculous but clean, quick closing, with an all cash offer, at about one third the original listing price. I was shocked when their counter was within $5K of my submission, so we settled on a split and completed the purchase. We off-loaded virtually everything from our RV, put in new wood floors and a new kitchen and headed back to Victoria to sell the truck and trailer. From then on we were out of the RV world, and would no longer need a truck to drive to California. The following season we completed all our planned renovations and the house turned into a beautiful gem. We got an additional bonus by finding other "snowbirds" as well as full time resident neighbors in our little community who have become very good friends.

Self-dentistry:

One evening when Allan was in Hemet for a visit, we were sitting in the living room watching TV and eating ice cream, when my tongue detected a noticeable change in a lower front tooth. It felt like a corner of the top of the tooth was suddenly missing. I asked Allan to verify the cause of this very uncomfortable feeling had just occurred. He looked at it and confirmed that the corner of the tooth was gone! Aside from the realization that I'd just eaten my own tooth, I knew my tongue was not going to get use to this feeling so I had to find a solution fast. I went to the bathroom, got one of Marcia's compact make-up mirrors, then went to my office, sat down and began the remediation process. When Allan heard the high-speed whining sound coming from my office he asked Marcia in the kitchen, what was that noise? Marcia said it sounded like Dennis is using his Dremel. Fortunately I had this rarely used tool. A Dremel is a small hand held high-speed rotary grinder used on metal, wood or plastic projects. With Marcia's mirror, I could now see the work that needed to be done. So I ground the remaining raised portion of the tooth down to the level of the break. Another problem fixed, and fast too!

12-12-12

Since we were living in the apartment on the ocean, our house on Cameo had both the main floor and lower suite rented, and while we were in the U.S. for the winters Shawn would handle any of the rental emergencies that arose. There came a time when the main floor of Cameo was going to have a turnover and Shawn was going to handle the showings etc., when he asked if I would consider selling the house, because he and his long time girlfriend Tina were interested in buying. Marcia and I were happy to help them move forward, so they bought it and did a wonderful job of renovating. The house had a separate entrance storage basement of nearly 1000

square feet, full of my old tools, and various parts and pieces for rental property repairs as well as junk I had been storing for both Brant and Shawn for the previous dozen years. Shortly after we returned to Victoria and Shawn and Tina were comfortably moved in, I got a call from Shawn asking me to come and pick the things I wanted to keep from the 'junk' in the storage area. When I got there he had already unloaded everything out onto the driveway! I told him I had planned to divide everything into 3 piles: Dump, Sell and Donate. He asked me to pick the things I intended to sell. I picked out a few items, then he asked what I thought I'd get for the entire bunch, and looked at me like I should think about the time and effort that pittance
would net. It was obvious there only needed to be two piles. We dumped and donated everything that afternoon, and I was glad for the release from the shackles of endlessly dragging junk.

In early December, while we were in California, we got a call from Shawn saying he and Tina were going to get married! They had been together for nearly 10 years, so it came as a surprise, and even more surprising was it was going to happen in a few days! It was obvious we would not be able to attend, but Shawn and Tina had planned that only her mother and his grandmother, my mother Margaret would be present. So on December 12, 2012 they had a JP come to their house and perform the ceremony witnessed by the two matriarchs, but the amazing part was that Shawn had a video camera set up to record the wedding and he Skyped it live to Brant in Los Angeles where he and his family watched on a laptop, which faced another laptop that Skyped it live to us in Hemet!

When we got back to Victoria in the spring, we had a big wedding party for Shawn and Tina at our yacht club. About two years later another surprise: their daughter Sydney was born. We now have four grand kids; two boys, two girls, two Canadians and two Americans!

Changing Cars Midstream

One winter, I bought a Volkswagen bug Cabriolet convertible in Palm Springs and brought it back to Victoria with a tow dolly.

It was cute but pretty much a 'girlie-car,' and as luck would have it, one lovely Sunday spring morning coming back from downtown after dropping off a couple that had come for a visit, I drove up beside a beautiful red Mitsubishi Spyder convertible. We both had our roofs down so I said to the other gray-haired owner that I loved the look of his car. That's when he told me he was the original owner and that due to new developments in his life, he was going to sell it! I asked him to pull off at the next street; I followed and parked behind him. I walked over to his door while assessing the exterior, asked the mileage and looked down at the interior, which was all mint. He told me the details of always keeping it in the garage because he walked to work most days, which explained the extraordinarily low miles, and now he just purchased a new Harley motorcycle, moved in with his girlfriend, and had no place to park this car.

I made him a cash offer on the spot and he accepted! He said, "Wow, this is pretty unusual, and I need to get home, so how about we do all the paperwork tomorrow." I agreed and we exchanged contact information. When I got home a few minutes later, I said, "Hey Marcia, you'll never guess what I just bought." She casually, but seriously said, "Is it a house?" When I told her the details she was excited at seeing it. I called Shawn to tell him, and he asked if it was a standard or automatic. That's when I realized I hadn't even sat in the car, let alone driven it! I thought I better clarify the transmission issue because I really didn't want a standard. By now the guy was home so I called him. When I told him on the phone that I was the guy that was going to buy his car, I'm sure he thought I had been straightened out by my wife and was phoning to cancel, however when he confirmed it was an automatic and I said, "OK, see you tomorrow."

He showed up the next day and I said, "I guess I should test drive it." I drove it 50 yards to the end of the cul-de-sac and back. We completed the deal, he took his plates off and as I walked him out of our underground parkade, I saw he looked a little dazed and was shaking his head. He said nothing like this had ever happened in his life and he still couldn't believe it!

It has turned out to be one of the best cars, of the nearly two hundred I've owned!

Though this seemed to be the quickest purchase, and shortest test-drive in my car history, it does not take first place!

The cramped travelling in our Toyota Matrix inspired me to stop by the Toyota dealer and ask for a trade-in value in case I wanted to make a change. When I got home, I called the sales manager at Toyota, who is a member of our golf club. I asked if he had a new Venza Limited in stock. He said one arrived just that morning. I had never been in a Venza, but both Marcia and I had seen them, liked the look and knew the 'Limited' model comes with every luxury item as standard and therefore had no options except paint color. I made him a cash offer for the trade-in difference. He agreed, so I told him we'd be in to see him in an hour or so with a check. He said, "It will be ready. I'll get it prepped right now." I didn't tell Marcia where we were going, so she was very surprised when we pulled into the dealership. I handed him the check, we signed the papers and just as that was completed we saw them bring it around to the front, still wet from its first wash. We went out to look at it and transfer our stuff from the Matrix to the Venza; we got in it for the first time and drove home.

From Water to Green

We loved living on the water watching the COHO Ferry, cruise ships, boats and floatplanes going in and out of the harbor, but the building was old. A few years earlier, I had put in a new bathroom, kitchen and wood flooring, but it only had one bathroom and the rest of the building was old and dark. I wanted to get something more modern, but I knew how much Marcia liked living on the water, and since we no longer had a boat for the first time in 30 years, making a change was going to be a challenge.

I started looking for a more modern condo but it had to be in a really great location or I'd never be able to sell the idea of moving. We knew that anything we considered had to be modern with two bedrooms, two bathrooms and secure parking with two spots. A view was important but facing south was critical. We looked at many options including high-rise views and other waterfronts, however there was always something wrong or missing.

We finally stumbled on a condo in the Ironwood complex located on the 1st fairway of the Gorge Vale Golf Course near downtown Victoria. This one had it all, so we set out to get it and we did. It was in perfect condition, but nothing had been changed or upgraded since its construction about seven years earlier. We repainted, put in new lighting, wood floors, crown moldings, solid countertops with tile backsplash, all new up-scale appliances, and moved in.

We were surprised to find that this significant change in view was an easy adjustment because when it is a gray, cloudy or rainy day on the water, it is a truly grey day, but we live one foot off the fairway and our view is green grass and trees, which stay green even on gray days! In fact we have to go out and put our hand out beyond the deck roof to know if it is raining!

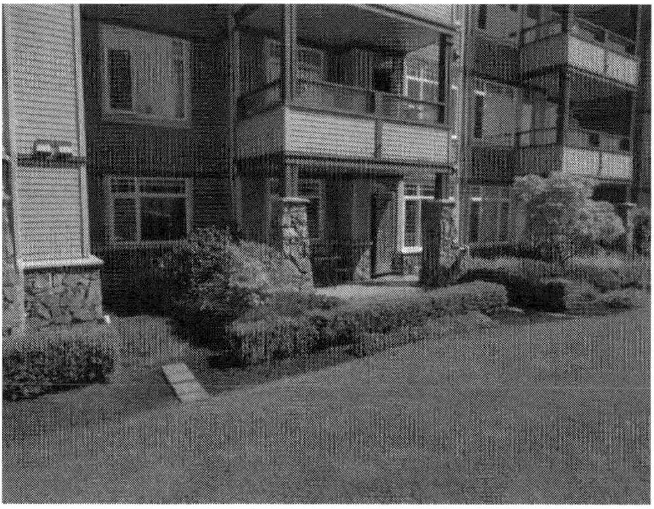

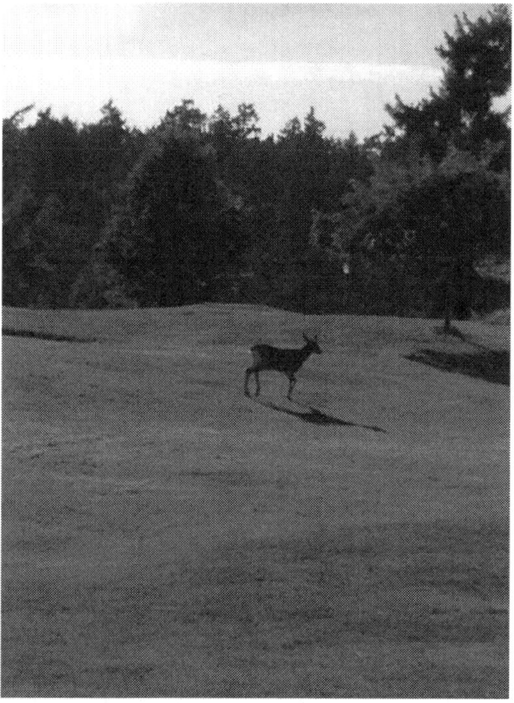

I had let my membership at Cedar Hill Golf Course lapse when we began going south for the winters and I was playing golf once a week at Cordova Bay, but now I was living right on the Gorge Golf Course. I went in to see the Gorge GM to see if there was any kind of deal we could work out that would make sense for me joining the Gorge and then be away half the year. When I came back and told Marcia there was no deal available, so I wouldn't be joining, she said, "Are you nuts! You play golf, and live on one of the nicest courses anywhere, and you're not going to join! Are you nuts?" Well obviously my frugal bones had once again, hopefully temporarily, overpowered my pea-brain. I joined Gorge Vale and quickly got involved with a group of about 35 seniors that play a few times a week. What a great group! The camaraderie of this diverse bunch of guys is something I look forward to every time I play. The fact that I'm away through the winter and still pay for the year anyway, makes this membership nearly twice as expensive, but now that I'm part of it, I know it's worth much more to me.

The Swell Factor:

After a day or so of rain, the conditions on the golf course were quite wet and slippery. I was walking down the cart path from the fifteenth tee box with three other guys, and just as I stepped onto the fairway, both feet went straight up in front of me. I fell backward, half way on the fairway and the concrete cart path. There was so much pain to go around, between my tailbone, back and ribs and right hand, that I didn't know which was worse.

Then I looked down at my hand and saw a very strange sight. In the fall, my right arm automatically went back to help break the fall, but as my hand hit the concrete, my ring finger took all the force and it bent it 90 degrees at the knuckle over my little finger. I had never seen anything like that before; half of one finger pointing in a totally different direction! I figured I'd have to go straight to the hospital, but thought it would be strange walking in with a hand looking like that, so instinctively just grabbed the end of my finger and pulled it over to align it with the others. To my surprise it snapped right back into place! Now a trip to the hospital immediately became a lower priority. In fact, I decided to pass on the hospital entirely, opting to finish playing the last four holes, as they were on the way back to the clubhouse anyway!

I was sure glad this wasn't going to interfere with our plans for a visit the next day with Mark arriving from Florida and Allan from Vancouver.

Unfortunately by the time my brothers arrived, my ring finger had swollen to about three times its normal size. It looked like an inflated balloon tied on the end of a pencil because I had not taken my ring off! When it first happened I thought the initial swelling would just go down and everything would be fine, but the ring was cutting off the circulation and my finger was blue.

When my brothers showed up, it was clear we had to get that ring off. It turned out to be a three-man job! I was able to slip the end of a teaspoon handle between my finger and the top of the ring. Allan snapped a vise grip plier onto the bottom edge of the ring to hold it stable. I held my hand steady with the other hand and Mark took the hacksaw and carefully made the strokes needed to cut through the ring using the teaspoon handle as a shield for my finger. Finally the ring broke, we pried it apart, freeing the ballooned finger, and no blood was shed!

The Mobile Tombstone

My dad had died in 1989 of congestive heart failure at the age of 76 leaving my mom Margaret a widow at age 65.

She lived alone at their condo until she was nearly 92 but it was becoming dangerous for her to be on her own at that age, especially since she was confined to a wheelchair. She was happy to get a nice one-bedroom unit at West Shore Lodge, an independent living facility that provided all the meals, linens, laundry and cleaning services, so to mom it was like living in a 5-star resort.

In Feb. 2018 mom turned 95!

The siblings got her condo ready for sale, which was a big job, but mom was very proud of the fact that she never had to go back to take care of those details. I was dealing with the actual sale of her condo and the day before the official closing, I got a call from the realtor saying there was a brick left on the deck. I didn't remember seeing one, and wondered why I would get a call about a "brick," so I went over to look. There it was a grey brick lying on its side up against the wall in the corner of the deck. It was much bigger and a lot heavier than a brick because it was a granite tombstone!

Dad was in the army in WW2 and had a small pension from Veterans Affairs, so when he died, they delivered an engraved granite tombstone to Mom. By the time she received it, we had already spread his ashes and purchased a brass plaque mounted at the foot of a tree in Saxx Point Park, where mom and dad spent nearly every summer day together for lunch. So mom simply put it on her deck where it stayed unnoticed and had been forgotten for decades. Now that I had it, I thought it would be nice to have it placed somewhere a little closer to our condo, so when family came to our place to visit we could see it easily. While playing on our golf course, I had seen several memorial plaques under trees, so it seemed fitting to pick a tree and mount it in the ground on the golf course near our ground level deck.

I considered asking for permission as Marcia suggested but chose to take the shortcut. After all I figured it is easier to beg for forgiveness than ask for permission. As luck would have it, there was a small tree about 40 feet on a diagonal from our door. Marcia always has better sense about most things than I do, and when I told her my plan to cut out the grass and fit it in as if it had been there for years, she was convinced it was not a good idea, so I compromised and did it at night! I was very proud of my handiwork because it looked like it had always been there and I was anxious to show it to the family. The next day I got a call from the GM at the golf course and he asked if I could come in to see him. I am one of the course ambassadors that promote membership so I'd been to see him several times before and expected him to tell me I was responsible for another new member joining. When I got to his office about 2 minutes after his call, as I walked in, I noticed he had a slightly more serious look on his face, and due to my many years of getting in trouble, I recognized something was wrong and there was a good chance I had something to do with it! Also with my many years in sales and reading body language, I asked if I should close the door. He said, "Yes!"

All those times in school where I'd been called into the principal's office to get punished for something I'd done, came flooding back!

He asked, "Did you put a tombstone in front of a tree recently?" Knowing this is not a question that someone asks out of the blue, my confession came immediately. He told me that he had received a complaint from the widow of a former course member. Her application to have a plaque installed on the course for her late husband had been rejected due to a changed policy some twelve years earlier, so they had planted a tree in his honor in front of her condo. Well I had just imbedded my dad's tombstone at the base of "her tree," and she was my next-door neighbor!

I apologized to the GM and told him I would remove it immediately, however the missing turf might be a problem. He assured me his grounds people would fix it. I went straight back and dug it up; then went over to profusely apologize to my neighbor. The next day the crew fixed the hole so there was no trace of my stupidity remaining. I thought, well, I have to find a better place, and why not on the beach at Saxx Point, after all if I could find a place there to insert it, and nobody would know that it hadn't been there for many years. I chose a cloudy weekday morning to go to the park when I knew there would be few observers to see me carry the big stone and shovel to the beach. When I got there, I found that I had forgotten that the 'beach' was actually just big rocks all the way into the water! But I came to do a job, and it was going to get done! I wandered from the beach toward the park itself until I found a very secluded, even somewhat hidden area that had some actual dirt, so I cut out a perfect fit and inserted the stone. It really looked like it had been there since the 80's. I went home feeling very satisfied.

About 4 months later, Mom called me in California and asked if I had put Dad's tombstone in Saxe Point? I told her about it when I installed it, but she had obviously forgotten, so I asked why she was wondering? She said some city workers had just delivered it to her, at the West Shore seniors' complex! I told her I would deal with it when I got back in the spring.

In the mean time I told the siblings about the ongoing saga, and Mark asked if he could have it for his house in Florida. I had been going to Florida every year for several years, so I told him I'd bring it with me on my next visit.

I usually only take carry-on luggage when I fly, and this hunk of granite took up most of my bag. It weighed over 40 pounds, and I knew that could be a problem in the airport. Fortunately I am quite strong so when I carried it, I made it appear to be as light as any other reasonable carry-on, however when I was going through the baggage screening it was quickly detected as something very, very strange. An agent was summoned over to inspect it as it rolled to the end of the track. He grabbed the handle and his body moved toward the table, but the bag and his hand stayed right there! He nearly pulled his arm out of its socket, and said, "Wow! What the hell is this?" I said, "A tombstone." He went back with both hands and strained to lift it to the table where he opened the zipper on my baggage. In reverent shock, he said, "OH! I'm so sorry, is a relative?" I said, "It's my dad, but he died in 1989!" His look changed to confusion, then he simply said, "OK, carry on." I still had to make it look reasonably light when boarding the plane to avoid drawing the attention of the attendants. It was quite a trick making it look light when I lifted it into the overhead compartment, but I got it to

Florida and it has finally found a home where Mark proudly displays it in his flower garden.

In Closing

This book chronicles only a part of the ups and downs in our journey so far, and it would be correct to say we've lived a charmed life, however it is important to note that it would not have been possible without the hard work and commitment Marcia and I shared as one. Looking back, I sometimes wish I could have been more mature at an earlier age, and wonder what could have been if I had been able to apply myself and get a good education. But those thoughts are not realistic because I was what I was, and I could not change that. I've had a good ride so far and really have no regrets, or a "Bucket List."

I recognize and greatly appreciate the wonderful family we have and the unconditional support Marcia has always provided for me, which allowed us to continually move forward in spite of some setbacks that might have sunk others.

We met as teens, a friend of her brother
but she knew at once there would be no other.
It wasn't long when it became clear to me
how important in my life this woman would be.

But the kid in me hung around for a while
so the first few years were a bit of a trial.
Some bad I did, though intent was not a part
and the good she saw through the eyes of her heart.

We started from scratch to share our life
and grew up together as husband and wife.
Our lives expanded from two to four
our sons Brant and Shawn, now we have more.

As a family we had more than most are blessed
though our love through their teens was truly a test.
We managed unscathed to weather the storms
but faded our showing of love in other forms.

Over time we allowed our lives to drift
couldn't seem to stop the inevitable rift.
So I set out with hope to chart a blind course
that would lead to eventual lingering remorse.

Separate and apart was the net result
but for each inner person was a sad assault.
Yet us together was her undaunted vision
while for me it was the qualm of my decision.

With help from our family and mostly our sons
we saw for each other no other ones.
This chance for us, for caring of a new kind
is due to the strength of her heart and mind.

I'm so grateful to have had our life so far
and will gladly work to raise the bar.
I am thankful for us and our future again
and happy forever to be Marcia's Den.

We've had great outcomes and lots of fun, but one thing is for sure; all the shortcuts I took along the way made the journey just as long! I'm glad I saw the opportunities and had some luck to help me through the mistakes and the learning. Now, it's too late for me, save yourself!

###

Acknowledgements:

Thanks to my mom and dad for providing a home of constant, unconditional love and stability.

My sons Brant and Shawn who helped immensely in the format and production.

My late cousin Brad Wolfe, who taught me to be an entrepreneur.

Louise Butcher, my brother Allan and sister Margot were great editors

Thanks to my sibs Mark and Dianne for their continued support.

Manufactured by Amazon.ca
Bolton, ON